Pre-Teen and Teenage Pregnancy

Also of interest from M&K Publishing.

Books can be ordered online at: www.mkupdate.co.uk

SKILLS FOR CARING SERIES
Self-directed study workbooks that will appeal to everyone with a health and social care interest. They can be used as a stand-alone modules or part of an assessment programme, or as part of a more formal training programme at a college or in the workplace. They have been designed to be very flexible.

Interpersonal Skills Workbook
ISBN: 978-1-905539-37-6

Loss and Grief Workbook
ISBN: 978-1-905539-43-7

Improving Patient Outcomes
ISBN: 978-1-905539-06-2

"This book does exactly what it sets out to do, it is clear, well written and written at the right level for the intended audience."

Directorate Manager, Merseyside

Improving Patient Outcomes is aimed at ward and department leaders and prospective leaders. The evidence for effective team working and its impact on patient care is readily available and as a leader you do not have to make enormous changes to the way you work to have an effect.

Visit the M&K website for a full listing of titles in print and forthcoming books.

A sample of forthcoming titles :

Aquatic Exercise for Pregnancy
ISBN: 978-1-905539-42-0

Managing Emotions in Women's Health
ISBN: 978-1-905539-07-9

Healthcare Management in Practice: an introductory guide
ISBN: 978-1-905539-33-8

Legal Principles and Clinical Practice
ISBN: 978-1-905539-32-1

Pre-Teen and Teenage Pregnancy

A twenty-first century reality

edited by
June L. Leishman and James Moir

ISBN: 978-1-905539-11-6

First published 2007

British Library Catalogue in Publication Data
A catalogue record for this book is available from the British Library

Notice:
Clinical practice and medical knowledge constantly evolve. Standard safety precautions must be followed, but, as knowledge is broadened by research, changes in practice, treatment and drug therapy may become necessary or appropriate. Readers must check the most current product information provided by the manufacturer of each drug to be administered and verify the dosages and correct administration, as well as contraindications. It is the responsibility of the practitioner, utilising the experience and knowledge of the patient, to determine dosages and the best treatment for each individual patient. Neither the publisher nor the authors assume any liability for any injury and/or damage to persons or property arising from this publication.
The Publisher

To contact M&K Publishing write to:
M&K Update Ltd · The Old Bakery · St. John's Street
Keswick · Cumbria CA12 5AS

Tel: 01768 773030 · Fax: 01768 781099
publishing@mkupdate.co.uk
www.mkupdate.co.uk

Designed & typeset in 11pt Usherwood Book by Mary Blood
Printed in England by Reed's) Ltd, Penrith, Cumbria.

Contents

Preface

Childhood and teenage pregnancy continues to pose significant social and health concerns within the UK and beyond. It is an issue that has implications for individuals across a range of professions and disciplines.

This book provides an insight into the social reality of sexually active young people in the UK today. It presents current research and contemporary professional practice related to pre-teen and teenage pregnancy and early age sexual activity and should be of interest to all professionals who work with young people, including nurses, midwives, doctors, social workers, teachers and community workers. The contributors all have first-hand experience of the reality of childhood and adolescence in the twenty-first century and acknowledge the risks of, and concerns about, early age sexual activity, pregnancy and childbirth, as well as the particular challenges faced by people working with the children and adolescents involved.

The book outlines the extent and scope of the problem nationally and internationally. It presents a social construction of contemporary childhood and adolescence and an overview of current research and practice in this area as experienced by the contributors.

How to use this book

This book is written for student nurses, midwives, doctors, social workers and teachers, as well as students of sexual and reproductive health and welfare, and highlights some of the issues faced by sexually active young people and those who work with them. We hope it may also be useful to general readers with a broad interest in the area, or the topic of particular chapters, which are structured to allow readers to 'dip into' topics as necessary. However we would encourage readers to read the book as a whole for a broader understanding of the issues.

The contributors

Jason Annetts PhD

Jason Annetts is a lecturer and the Sociology Division Leader at the University of Abertay, Dundee and teaches modules on health, sexuality and social movements and political protest. His current research interests are focused on sex education and he has just completed a Scottish Executive-funded report on the support needs of teachers delivering sex and relationships education in primary schools.

Elizabeth Kennedy MB, ChB, MSc, MFFP, MIPM, MRCGP

Elizabeth Kennedy graduated from Glasgow University in 1980 and trained for general practice. After working as a principal in the Glasgow area, she moved to Tayside and is now an Associate Specialist in Family Planning and the Lead Clinician for the Tayside service.

She has always been interested in women's health and sexual health and undertook an MSc in Community Gynaecology and Reproductive Healthcare at Warwick University in 2002. She represents Tayside and Scotland on various Faculty of Family Planning Committees and she has an interest in young people's sexual health and in psychosexual medicine.

Theo Kwansa PhD, MEd, MTD, Dip Nurse (CT), RGN, RM, ADM

Theo Kwansa is currently the Advisor of Studies for students in the School of Social and Health Sciences at the University of Abertay, Dundee. Her teaching includes research methods, gender studies and contemporary issues in nursing and care. She is a registered midwife and has worked extensively in the field of sexual and reproductive health education for over a decade. Her research interests are in healthcare education, student self-direction and learning styles, as well as changing trends in maternal and infant care. She has published in peer-reviewed journals and presented at international conferences.

Jan Law

Jan Law is a tutor in sociology at the University of Abertay. She has also been involved in various research projects in relation to areas of poverty, social exclusion and health and has recently completed three research projects in these areas at Dundee University: including one on people who self-neglect and another on access to healthcare for people who are homeless and disabled. In addition, she has also just completed a Scottish Executive-funded review of the child protection reform programme.

June L. Leishman PhD, MEd (Hons), Post Grad Dip Ed, Cert HE Psychology, Cert HE Social Psychology RNT RCNT RMN

June Leishman is Director of Operations in the School of Social and Health Sciences at the University of Abertay, Dundee. She is a registered nurse, registered clinical nurse educator and registered nurse teacher and prior to her academic career she worked with a diverse range of client groups across a range of clinical settings. She did her doctorate in Social Sciences and Health and has published in peer-reviewed professional journals and presented at conferences across the world. She contributes to the delivery of courses on sexual and reproductive health, gender issues in healthcare, research methods and concepts in mental health education and practice.

She is a Winston Churchill Fellow, a Florence Nightingale Scholar and, for services to nurse education, was invited to become a member of Sigma Theta Tau International.

James Moir PhD, MEd (Hons), BEd

James Moir is Director of Academic Programmes in the School of Social and Health Sciences at the University of Abertay, Dundee. He is a sociologist with a research interest in the application of discourse analysis: the analysis of the construction of 'objects' in spoken, written and visual texts. His research has included: the construction of occupational identities in conversation, particularly in relation to nursing and healthcare occupations; doctor-patient interaction and shared decision-making; discourses of reading 'body language'; representations of the 'mind' in film and television; talk about 'responsibility' in relation to environmental concerns; the representation of 'opinions' in political opinion polling; gender 'work-life balance' talk; and the construction of 'child development' in terms of how children talk. A recurring theme is an examination of discursive psychology and how people relate the 'inner world' of mind to an 'outer world' that requires to be perceived and understood.

Dianna Reed MB, ChB, DRCOG, MRCGP, MFFP

Dianna Reed graduated from Aberdeen University in 1993 and initially trained in general practice, changing career in 1998 to work in the Department of Family Planning in Dumfries. There she combined this specialism with community paediatrics until 2003 when she decided to concentrate on the field of sexual health.

She represents family planning in Tayside on various committees including clinical governance and cervical screening. Currently undergoing training in psychosexual medicine, she has a particular interest in young people's sexual health.

Chapter 1
Introduction
June L. Leishman

Definitions of adolescence vary between different societies, but for the purpose of this book, the terms 'adolescents', 'young people' and 'youth' are used interchangeably. We have taken the United Nations Population Fund (UNPFA, 2001) definition of adolescence, commonly regarded as the period between childhood and adulthood, as the period between ten years and 19 years of age, as our reference for the population at the centre of our discussions. According to the Marie Stopes International Organisation (2007), it is this age group that makes up over half the world's population and many of them are sexually active, despite limited knowledge or understanding of sex, reproductive health risks or their consequences.

Adolescence is a time when young people begin to develop their individual identity and social relationships. It is also a time when they begin to engage in 'risk-taking' behaviours and suffer the consequences of these behaviours – 'risk outcomes'. At the same time they are often facing exams and educational and career choices, all of which make adolescence complex and challenging. According to the World Health Organisation (WHO, 2000), the needs of children and adolescents remain poorly understood and served in much of the world and the WHO stresses the far-reaching consequences for society of this failure. Resnick and Burt (1996) identify health risk behaviours in young people as voluntary behaviours that threaten the wellbeing of teenagers and limit their potential for achieving responsible adulthood. Duberstein Lindberg *et al.* (2000) in their statistical portrait of teenage risk-taking cite ten common behaviours that adolescents commonly engage in, either in an exploratory way or more regularly. These include alcohol use, binge drinking, tobacco and substance use, physical fighting, weapon carrying, attempted suicide and sexual risk-taking (that is, unprotected sexual activity).

Pre-teen and teenage pregnancy

Policymakers and researchers in the UK tend to see pre-teen and teenage pregnancy as the risk outcome of sexual risk-taking. In 1999, the government launched a ten-year Teenage Pregnancy Strategy, the main aims of which were to halve conceptions by under eighteens and establish a downward trend in conceptions by under sixteens by 2010. This has become one of the most significant public health challenges faced by government today and includes increasing the participation of teenage parents in education, training and employment to 60% by 2010 to reduce their risk of long-term social exclusion (Health Development Agency, 2004).

Despite records of decreasing conception rates over the last few years, the UK statistics are still high by comparison with other Western European countries and the UK is second only to the US in the western developed world (Office for National Statistics, 2001). As the WHO 2005 European Health Report identifies, teenage pregnancy and early parenthood can lead to poor educational achievement, poor physical and mental health, poverty and isolation for mothers and their children, with a particular emphasis on socio-economic disadvantage being both a cause and consequence of early parenthood (WHO, 2005). The extent of this problem and the related physical and psychological health consequences of early age sexual activity are addressed in more depth in Chapters 2 and 4, as are current trends in such threats to reproductive health as HIV/AIDS and sexually-transmitted diseases (STDs). In Chapter 5, Theo Kwansa surveys the issues related to the prescribing of contraceptives to teenagers and reproductive healthcare education.

Identifying teenage pregnancy as a social problem is in itself problematic. In analysing US and UK research literature on this topic, Bonnell (2004) contrasts the various justifications for social science research in this topic area. In the UK, the focus is more on the health consequences of early age sexual activity and pregnancy, while, in the US, teenage pregnancy and motherhood are seen as a problem because of their implications for government and welfare expenditure. These perspectives reflect cultural and political differences between the UK and the US. Many of the US studies also involved disadvantaged black females and appear to present a black 'ghetto' subculture perspective, which has social 'underclass' connotations and is highlighted in the longitudinal 'Baltimore Study' carried out by Furstenberg (2003). The link between the concept of 'underclass theory' and social exclusion in the UK is made in Davies' (2005) controversial paper on the Government's social inclusion strategy. It draws on the moral underclass discourses of Charles Murray (1990; 1994; 1989; 1999) and explores key areas of contention with regard to New Labour's approach to tackling social exclusion.

Early sexual activity is not a new phenomenon. It is both culturally and historically situated and is located within traditional concepts of marriage and family. It is not uncommon in some cultures for young girls to enter into marriage post puberty and to bear children in their teenage years. It is equally not new for adolescents to be sexually active and for teenage girls to become pregnant as a result. What has changed significantly over time is marriage by the young people involved as a result of early age pregnancy. In Chapter 3, James Moir explores the discourse of 'problematising' young people and argues for a more 'enlightened' approach that acknowledges the changing world of 'youth' as a series of social practices and relations within which sexual activity is located.

Much of the political discourse regarding social inclusion centres on collaboration and cooperation in professional public service delivery, with a significant emphasis on education. The concept of health-promoting schools is not a new one. However, sexual health promotion at primary school level is relatively new in the UK. New guidance on the teaching of sexual health and relationships education (SRE) was issued by the DfES in 2000 and there is evidence that school-based SRE is effective in delaying the age of onset of first intercourse, increasing condom use at first intercourse and reducing teenage pregnancies (Mellanby *et al.*, 1995).

The emphasis on beginning sexual health promotion in primary schools in Scotland reflects the Scottish Executive's concern about Scotland's teenage conception rate, which is the highest in the UK (Scottish Health Services, 1998). Throughout Scotland regional health and education authorities are working in partnership to address this important public health challenge and to comply with the National Sexual Health Strategy. The Strategy is built on the pillars of respect and responsibility and, for the first time in Scotland, presents a coherent framework for improving sexual health that is respectful of the rights of young people and parents and recognises personal responsibility as well as religious, cultural and gender diversity. In Chapter 6, Jason Annetts and Jan Law explore the obligations placed on, and advice given to, primary schools on sexual health and relationship teaching and consider the support that could be given to primary school teachers to enable them to fulfil their role as sexual health promoters.

In Chapters 7 and 8, Elizabeth Kennedy and Dianna Reed, both medical professionals actively involved with young people's reproductive health and the care of pregnant adolescents, present examples of some of the interventions that they are currently engaged in. They serve to illustrate the level of commitment of many practitioners to helping reduce the risk of early sexual activity and unplanned pregnancy in the future.

The work being done in Dundee is encouraging and significant at a local level, however it should be noted that in all other regions of the country, local authorities have their own sexual and reproductive health strategies in place. These are at various stages of development, not unlike the general landscape of sexual and reproductive health strategy developments across the UK as a whole. The message is clear in all these strategy reports. Key features of a successful sexual health strategy must include: integration in service provision, community involvement, education and training of professionals, youth-focused health promotion, cultural awareness and ease of access to services.

By presenting pre-teen and teenage pregnancy from a range of social, medical and healthcare perspectives, we hope to offer professionals and general readers a deeper understanding of this complex area and support better collaborative working to protect the sexual health and wellbeing of our teenagers.

References

Bonnell, C. (2004) Why is teenage pregnancy conceptualised as a social problem? *Culture, Health and Sexuality*, 6(3): 255–272.

Davies, J.S. (2005) The social exclusion debate: Strategies, controversies and dilemmas. *Policy Studies* 26(1): 3–27.

Duberstein Lindberg, L., Boggess, S., Porter, L. and Williams, S. (2000) *Teen Risk Taking: A statistical portrait* Washington DC: Urban Institute Office of Public Affairs.

Furstenberg Jnr, F.F. (2003) Teenage childbearing as a public issue and private concern. *Annual Review of Sociology* 29: 23–64.

Health Development Agency (2004) *Teenage Pregnancy: An overview of the research evidence by the Teenage Pregnancy Unit.*
Available at http://www.nice.org.uk (accessed May 2007).

Health Protection Agency (2006) *Chlamydia.*
Available at http://www.hpa.org.uk (accessed May 2007).

Marie Stopes International Organisation (2007) *Young people.*
Available at http://www.mariestopes.org.uk/ww/ (accessed May 2007).

Mellanby, A.R., Phelps, F.A., Chrighton, N.J. and Tripp, J.H. (1995) Schools Sex Education: An experimental programme with educational and medical benefit. *British Medical Journal* 311: 175–417.

Murray, C. (1990) *The Emerging British Underclass* London: IEA, Health and Welfare Unit.

Murray, C. (1994) *Underclass: The crisis deepens* London: IEA, Health and Welfare Unit.

Murray, C. (1998) *Income Equality and IQ* Washington DC: The American Institute Press.

Murray, C. (1999) *The Underclass Revisited.*
Available at http://www.aei.org/publications (accessed May 2007).

Office for National Statistics (2001) *Population Trends* London: ONS.

Resnick, G. and Burt, M.R. (1996) Youth at risk: Definitions and implications for service delivery. *American Journal of Orthopsychiatry* 66(2): 172–188.

Scottish Health Services (1998) *Teenage Pregnancy in Scotland: A 15 year review* Edinburgh: Information and Statistics Division, Common Services Agency.

UNFPA (2001) *Young People and Demographic Trends* Fact Sheet. New York: UNFPA.

WHO (2000) *Adolescent Sexual and Reproductive Health* Geneva: WHO, Department of Reproductive Health and Research (RHR).

WHO (2005) *The European Health Report 2005* WHO Regional Office for Europe.
Available at http://www.euro.who.int (accessed May 2007).

Chapter 2
The range and scope of early age sexual activity and pregnancy

June L. Leishman

The Marie Stopes International Organisation (2007) reports that over half the world's current population is made up of young people within the ten to nineteen age range, many of whom are sexually active despite limited knowledge or understanding of sex, reproductive health risks and the related consequences.

Teenage pregnancy is not a new phenomenon, culturally or historically. It is customary in some cultures for females to marry and give birth soon after menstruation begins. However, early marriage occurs more frequently in developing rather than developed countries, with a median age of marriage in South Asia of around sixteen years, seventeen years in sub-Saharan Africa, eighteen in Western Asia and nineteen in North Africa (Fathalla, 1994) and in many African countries, young people are sexually active at a much earlier age, frequently without the use of contraception (Ajayi *et al.*, 1991; Ageyi and Epema, 1992; Gorgen *et al.*, 1993). In some East Asian countries strong religious and political control discouraging premarital sexual activity may contribute to suppressing the levels of adolescent childbearing, but reliable data is unavailable on pregnancies, births or terminations.

Young girls are also subject to gender inequality in countries where early sexual activity and experience with a number of partners is viewed as a rite of passage for young men but not for young girls. This may lead girls to deny their sexual activity. In western societies, the incidences of early sexual intercourse and the numbers of pregnancies as a result of unprotected sex have increased sharply since World War II (WHO, 2004). Young males and females are sexually active significantly earlier than in previous decades, with many experiencing first intercourse while still in primary school.

Pre-teen and teenage pregnancy

In the UK, teenage pregnancy has become a significant public health issue and is central to the Government's strategy to prevent health inequalities, child poverty and social exclusion (Social Exclusion Unit, 1999). As such, it is an issue that has implications for healthcare practitioners and other professionals across a wide range of disciplines involved in the education, care and welfare of young people. This chapter aims to contextualise this problem both globally and nationally, illustrate the range and scope of the problem and identify briefly the risks of early sexual activity and pregnancy for young people. This provides a starting point for more in-depth discussions in later chapters from the point of view of experts in the fields of sociology, social sciences, medicine and healthcare. Finally, this chapter proposes that the social and healthcare needs of young people and issues related to sexual health are necessary components of any educational work with young people.

The global picture

The global picture

The recorded incidences of adolescent pregnancy and adolescent birth are widely divergent. For most countries, comparable figures are available on birth rates to mothers aged between fifteen and nineteen. Table 2.1 is based on UNICEF (1998) figures cited in a recent WHO report on adolescent pregnancy (WHO, 2006). These figures are based on birth registration rates and in most developed countries these figures are reliable. However, in some of the developing countries the data can only be based on best estimates available (Singh and Darroch, 2000). (See Table 2.1.)

The picture in the UK

The picture in the UK

Early age pregnancy in the UK remains problematic. Currently the UK teenage pregnancy rate is among the highest in Europe and second to the US in the western developed world (Royal Institute of Public Health, 2007). The UK rate is almost five times higher than Holland, four times higher than France and over twice that of Germany (Coombes, 2002). Of the four home nations, Scotland has the highest rate of teenage pregnancy (Scottish Health Service, 1998). The figures for England and Wales in 2003 in Table 2.2 are taken from National Statistics Quarterly 26 and 27 amendment data (2005) and the figures for Scotland have been taken from a Scottish Health Statistics release (2007). (See Table 2.2.)

Early age sexual activity and pregnancy

Table 2.1   **Births per 1000 females aged 15–19 years**

Sub-Saharan Africa		M. East & N. Africa		East/South Asia Pacific		Americas		Europe	
Mauritius	45	Tunisia	18	Japan	4	Canada	24	Switzerland	4
Rwanda	54	Israel	19	Korea Rep.	4	Chile	49	Netherlands	7
S. Africa	70	Algeria	24	China	5	Trinidad	51	France	8
Botswana	83	Lebanon	26	Korea Dem.	5	Haiti	53	Italy	8
Kenya	101	Morocco	28	Singapore	6	Peru	57	Belgium	9
Namibia	104	Kuwait	31	Cambodia	15	USA	60	Denmark	9
Zimbabwe	114	Turkey	43	Sri Lanka	20	Uruguay	64	Spain	10
Ghana	115	Jordan	44	Australia	22	Argentina	65	Sweden	10
Togo	119	Syria	44	Pap. N. Guin.	24	Cuba	65	Finland	11
Mozambique	124	Iraq	45	Malaysia	26	Mexico	69	Germany	13
Tanzania	124	Sudan	52	Myanmar	31	Brazil	71	Ireland	14
Eritrea	128	Egypt	62	N. Zealand	32	Ecuador	71	Norway	16
Zambia	132	U. Arab. Emir	73	Viet Nam	33	Colombia	74	Greece	18
C. Afr. Rep	134	Iran	77	Mongolia	39	Paraguay	76	Austria	21
Congo	136	Yemen	101	Philippines	40	Bolivia	79	Lithuania	22
Nigeria	138	Libya	102	Lao Rep	50	Panama	81	Portugal	24
Cameroon	140	Saudi Arabia	114	Indonesia	58	Dom. Rep.	88	Belarus	24
Madagascar	142	Oman	122	Thailand	70	Jamaica	88	Poland	25
Senegal	142			Bhutan	84	Costa Rica	89	Estonia	27
Gambia	153			Nepal	89	El Salvador	92	Slovenia	27
Burk. Faso	157			Pakistan	89	Venezuela	98	Bosnia Herz.	29
Malawi	159			India	109	Guatemala	111	Hungary	29
Ethiopia	168			Bangladesh	115	Honduras	113	Latvia	30
Chad	173					Nicaragua	133	Albania	31
Gabon	175							Croatia	31
Uganda	179							UK	31
Guinea Bis.	180							Moldova R.	32
Mali	181							Czech R.	35
Sierra Leo.	201							Slovakia	35
Congo D. R.	206							Ukraine	36
Liberia	206							Yugoslavia	38
Somalia	208							Russian Fd.	39
Angola	212							Macedonia	40
								Romania	43

Pre-teen and teenage pregnancy

Table 2.2   **Conceptions by age, 2002–3**

England and Wales

Under 14 yrs		14 yrs		15 yrs		16 yrs		17 yrs		18 yrs		19 yrs	
2002	2003	2002	2003	2002	2003	2002	2003	2002	2003	2002	2003	2002	2003
390	337	1858	1893	5627	5846	13475	13285	20601	20822	25910	26562	29246	29782

Scotland

Under 14 yrs		14 yrs		15 yrs		16 yrs		17 yrs		18 yrs		19 yrs	
2002	2003	2002	2003	2002	2003	2002	2003	2002	2003	2002	2003	2002	2003
24	14	146	155	489	510	1324	1270	1889	1964	2273	2330	2416	2508

Each year, around 56,000 babies are born to teenage mothers in Britain (Brennan, 2002). Much of the research shows that childbearing adolescents are susceptible to myriad health-related problems, including physiological and psychological problems which affect both their own and their children's lives. Suicide attempts, parenting problems, domestic violence, poor birth outcomes, and sexually transmitted diseases, including HIV, are among the diverse problems encountered.

Much good work is being done to roll out services for young people across the UK. In England this is much to the credit of the Teenage Pregnancy Unit. Alongside this, innovative approaches to working with young people are being taken across the whole of the UK by the Family Planning Association's projects with young people, such as Jiwsi and Ruby in Wales, Check it Out and Choices in Northern Ireland, the Wise Boy project in England and the Aw'right and Sexability projects in Scotland (FPA, 2006).

Consequences of unprotected early sexual activity

Early sexual activity

Early age pregnancy is usually a crisis for the pregnant girl and her family. The most common reactions include anger, guilt and denial and, if the father is also young, similar reactions occur in his family. The mother faces three options: continue with the pregnancy and keep the baby, continue with the pregnancy and have the baby adopted or terminate the pregnancy. Young mothers are also caught in a legal contradiction between their status as parents and their status as minors, and a conflict with the rights and responsibilities of the father. Pregnant young people require

Early age sexual activity and pregnancy

special understanding and sensitive healthcare and health education. Legge (2002) claims that nurses are fighting a huge battle for sexual health given the increasing rates of STDs and teenage pregnancy. According to the Marie Stopes International Organisation (2003), the known health risks for this age group include STDs, sexual violence, HIV infections, abortions in unsafe and illegal conditions and maternal mortality.

In 2006, we reached the twenty-fifth anniversary of the first reported case of acquired immunodeficiency syndrome (AIDS) and the beginning of HIV surveillance in the UK. Over the past 25 years, there has been unprecedented priority given to the control and management of HIV and STDs in the UK. HIV is a chronic infection with a long latent period. It predominantly affects younger adults. In the UK in 2005, 70% of cases were aged fifteen to 39 years at diagnosis. HIV is still incurable despite the introduction of new treatments and London, Brighton and Manchester have the highest infection rates (Health Protection Agency, 2006). For the UK as a whole, there were 82,700 cases of HIV infection and over 22,500 ongoing AIDS cases between 1 June 2006 and 20 September 2006 (Health Protection Scotland, 2006).

Despite improvements in health promotion and interventions such as screening of blood products, voluntary HIV testing and introduction of needle exchange schemes, HIV and other STDs remain a major public health concern in the UK. Data adapted from the Health Protection Agency (2006), in Table 2.3, shows the new diagnoses of STDs in young people in the UK over the last decade.

Table 2.3

New diagnoses of STDs by sex and age, 1996–2005

A. Syphilis (primary and secondary)

Males	1996	1997	1998	1999	2000	2001	2002	2003	2004	2005
< 15	1	3	0	0	0	0	1	0	0	3
15	0	0	0	0	0	0	0	0	1	1
< 16	1	3	0	0	0	0	1	0	1	4
16–19	4	1	5	7	8	12	29	33	35	79
Females										
< 15	0	0	0	0	0	0	2	0	0	8
15	0	0	0	0	1	1	1	3	2	5
< 16	0	0	0	0	1	1	2	3	2	13
16–19	4	5	3	13	9	14	17	23	30	34

B. Gonorrhoea (uncomplicated)

Males	1996	1997	1998	1999	2000	2001	2002	2003	2004	2005
< 15	12	24	7	14	18	10	16	20	11	15
15	23	24	30	31	43	48	52	40	43	37
< 16	35	48	37	45	61	58	68	60	54	52
16–19	930	1088	1050	1414	1954	2100	2283	2112	2001	1627
Females										
< 15	3	5	0	0	1	2	1	1	2	1
15	1	2	1	0	1	0	3	1	1	4
< 16	4	7	1	0	2	2	4	2	3	5
16–19	50	74	59	83	148	159	193	187	186	209

C. Genital chlamydia (uncomplicated)

Males	1996	1997	1998	1999	2000	2001	2002	2003	2004	2005
< 15	13	18	18	25	19	25	27	34	32	33
15	32	35	37	52	58	69	78	102	101	111
< 16	45	53	55	77	77	94	105	136	133	144
16–19	1511	1987	2570	3168	4008	4553	5661	6565	7602	8261
Females										
< 15	124	143	146	181	197	239	255	292	306	324
15	354	406	455	565	643	747	867	1053	1069	1010
< 16	478	549	601	746	840	986	1122	1345	1375	1334
16–19	6143	7952	9149	10908	12813	14307	16560	18502	20046	20976

D. Genital herpes (first attack)

Males	1996	1997	1998	1999	2000	2001	2002	2003	2004	2005
< 15	6	8	3	2	8	2	3	3	1	3
15	4	4	8	3	5	7	6	5	6	7
< 16	10	12	11	5	13	9	9	8	7	10
16–19	292	278	342	385	420	417	431	416	455	562
Females										
< 15	26	35	31	37	35	55	41	51	36	41
15	95	76	71	87	99	102	120	122	120	116
< 16	121	111	102	124	134	157	161	173	156	157
16–19	1784	1921	1992	2046	2117	2301	2170	2270	2360	2408

Early age sexual activity and pregnancy

E. Genital warts (first attack)

Males	1996	1997	1998	1999	2000	2001	2002	2003	2004	2005
<15	58	70	55	55	53	38	33	42	34	28
15	37	35	45	49	46	25	42	62	45	45
<16	95	105	100	104	99	63	75	104	79	73
16–19	2306	2836	3218	3548	3564	3629	3677	3997	4448	4521
Females										
<15	142	143	149	179	122	140	145	138	146	142
15	403	354	346	342	348	364	402	418	465	398
<16	545	497	495	521	470	504	547	556	601	540
16–19	8449	9168	9587	9461	9341	9500	9530	10026	10766	11261

There have been substantial changes in the epidemiology of HIV and other STDs over the past 25 years, and particularly the past decade. Rapid increases in acute STDs have placed significant pressures on sexual health services across the UK. Greater access to Genito-Urinary Medicine (GUM) clinics and further development of the role of the primary care sector are key requirements for the control and management of acute STDs, which are associated with substantial morbidity and mortality rates.

The need to reach individuals who remain undiagnosed and those most at risk of HIV and other STDs and target them with culturally sensitive and effective interventions presents an ongoing public health challenge. In its first National Strategy for Sexual Health and HIV, the Government recognised the serious consequences of poor sexual health and cited the number of visits to genito-urinary medicine clinics at over a million per year. This figure has doubled over the last decade (DH, 2001a). Johnson, in his paper on sexual behaviour in the UK, highlights the increase in STDs and HIV, with the diagnoses of chlamydia, gonorrhoea and syphilis having doubled in the last five years (Johnson, 2002). These concerns are reiterated in the Department of Health's Sexual Health and HIV Strategy report (DH, 2001b) which says that one in ten sexually active young men and women are infected with chlamydia and that HIV diagnoses have risen to an unprecedented 6,500. The long-term consequences of STDs present further problems for these young people in terms of potential infertility and chronic illnesses in later life. Coupled with this, there are issues related to the psychological health of young people as a result of early age pregnancy. As Whitehead highlights, the emotional experience of young women is frequently overlooked (Whitehead, 2001).

Mental health issues

Mental health issues

Lesser and Escoto-Lloyde (1999) report that teenage pregnancy has been cited as a trigger for a range of mental health problems, para-suicide and suicide in young people and adolescents, a fact confirmed by a recent report on child and adolescent mental health from the Public Health Institute of Scotland (2000). Logsdon (2004) also notes that depression is of particular concern in pregnant and postpartum adolescents because of the potential impact on the infant. As a consequence, primary care providers should routinely screen adolescent girls for depression and consider depression in their differential diagnoses of somatic complaints. Medication, psychotherapy and cognitive behavioural therapy are all effective treatments for depression in adolescents.

The correlation between unplanned pregnancy and adolescent suicide attempts is presented in McClain's Canadian study (2003). Langer's (2002) study of unplanned pregnancy focused on Latin America and the Caribbean. Both studies found that unwanted pregnancies especially affect adolescent single women, some of whom opt for an unsafe abortion, which can lead to their death. Langer also reports that such women may resort to suicide or be the victims of murder by a family member or another person who is unhappy that the pregnancy has occurred. Similarly, severe depression and attempted suicide, suicide and honour killings form part of the landscape of early age pregnancy in the UK.

In a seven-year follow-up investigation of women who were pregnant as teenagers, Turner *et al.* (2000) identified that, consistent with other research, differences in social support and in personal resources or attributes played a key factor in influencing the psychological condition or adaptation of young mothers. Foote (1997) highlights the need for professionals to develop particular sensitivity and relationship-building skills when working with these vulnerable young people and their families.

Early age sexual activity and pregnancy

Legal issues

Further complicating these physical and psychological issues are the legal implications of under-age sexual activity (Dimond, 2002).

Under the Sexual Offences Amendment Act (The Stationery Office, 2000), sexual activities for young people under sixteen years old are prohibited. Therefore, in theory, if the law were to be followed, teenagers and pre-teen girls should not be getting pregnant at all. Wellings (2001) highlights the fact that despite many of these young people knowing that it is illegal to have intercourse prior to the age of sixteen, many are sexually active long before that age with the majority of that sexual activity consensual and therefore difficult to enforce legislation against. However, young people are also vulnerable to pressure to engage in sexual activities, exploitation and abuse. There have been fewer studies on this in the UK than in the US (Kennedy *et al.*, 1997; Harner, 2004), but the recent change in UK law to increase the penalty for internet child 'grooming', would suggest that there are concerns about child abuse in this country. To complicate the legal situation further, the Human Rights Act (HMSO, 1998) brings into play an individual young person's right to self-determination, right to refuse treatment, right to decide about termination and right to confidentiality.

Abortion

Abortion in the UK is legal under the 1967 Abortion Act, where two registered medical practitioners form the opinion 'on good faith' that the pregnancy has not exceeded its twenty-fourth week and that the continuance of the pregnancy would involve risk of injury to the physical or mental health of a pregnant woman or any of her existing children (Lee, 1999). An abortion can also be performed at any gestational age where there is a substantial risk that if the child were born it would be severely handicapped (Sheldon, 1997). It remains a highly controversial subject across society, the legal and healthcare professions (Sheldon, 1997; Herring, 1997; Jackson, 2003).

Abortion is commonplace in the UK. In 2005, the number of abortions for women resident in England and Wales was 186,400 compared with 185,700 in 2004. In Scotland, the figure was 12,461 in 2004 compared with 12,603 in 2005. In 2005 in

Pre-teen and teenage pregnancy

England and Wales there were just over 1,000 abortions carried out on girls under fifteen years old and in 2003–5 there were a total of 33 abortions carried out on girls under thirteen years old and 409 to girls aged thirteen years old. In Scotland, abortions in the under twenty years age group were 3218 in 2005, compared with 3304 in 2004 (DH, 2006; Scottish Health Statistics, 2006).

Davey (2005) finds that, despite improvements in NHS-funded abortion services and new recommended standards for sexual health and HIV services, waiting times for abortion remain too long. Abortion has also never been extended to Northern Ireland.

Social exclusion

Social exclusion

Much of the thinking around the complex issue of early age sexual activity and pregnancy appears to situate the problem within a cycle of social exclusion.

Social exclusion often begins in childhood, with poor parenting, truancy and disrupted education. The effects can be catastrophic, for the individual and for society, and are commonly implicated in mental illness and criminal behaviour in adulthood. Studies show that rates of crime, suicide and unexpected death are highest among the most excluded, but also that the cycle of disadvantage can be broken by early, practical intervention (Pritchard and Mason, 2000). One school of thought suggests that whilst teenage pregnancy can be the result of disadvantage and social exclusion, it can also lead to social exclusion for young people whose education and career prospects are affected as a result of unplanned pregnancy.

In the National Health Service Plan (DH, 2000) the Government's focus is on health priorities and putting patients at the heart of the health service. This includes pinpointing the changes that are most urgently needed to improve individual health and wellbeing. School truancy, teenage pregnancy and sleeping rough are some of the big social issues being addressed as a result. Alongside the ultimate goal of halving conceptions among under eighteens by 2010, is the desire to achieve a reduction in the risk of long-term social exclusion for teenage parents and their children.

Policymakers might help to reduce these risks by improving access to high quality information and services with the creation of health-enabling environments that facilitate young people's efforts to protect and enhance their sexual health. This gap in service provision was identified in the Social Exclusion Unit's Teenage Pregnancy report (1999). Sex education for this population is controversial with varying opinions from religious groups and parents. Given its complexity, professionals working with young people and adolescents must equip themselves with a wide range of practical and interpersonal skills, as well as extensive knowledge of the issues and the current legislation.

Learning about sex and relationships is a lifelong process, which starts early. For most young people, parents are their first influence and research indicates that a positive home environment where there is open discussion about sexuality can act as a protective factor in young people's sexual activity, and in the prevention of teenage pregnancy (Wellings and Field, 1996). Within families, a number of aspects have been found to influence the sexual behaviours of young people, including the characteristics of the parents, the family structure, relationships and interactions (Fullerton, 2005). Burford views families as agents and architects of civil society and social inclusion, and suggests that government should do all that it can to both support and foster this family orientated social inclusion role (Burford, 2005).

Strategies to provide better education and services to young people to combat teenage pregnancy include contraceptive services that can be easily accessed by young people, including those who are still at school, and a more robust approach to health promotion in schools (Allen and Bradley, 2001). All schools in the UK are expected to provide sexual health and relationship education (SRE), presenting facts in an objective, balanced and sensitive manner within a framework of sound values. Jason Annetts and Jan Law address the role of sexual health education in schools further in Chapter 6.

The role of healthcare professionals

The role of professionals

Much of the rhetoric on sexual health service provision for young people focuses on access in schools. Sutton, in her paper on sexual health promotion in schools, views the school nurse role as vital for reducing the pregnancy rates in the UK (Sutton, 2001). This is supported by Crouch (2002) who suggests that school nurses might play a significant role in meeting the Government's 'better prevention' agenda and Perry (2002) highlights the role that midwives could play in educating for prevention and birth control and helping to deal with the psychosocial implications of early age pregnancy. Smith (1997) also suggests that nurses involved in adolescent healthcare can help reduce STDs by focusing on disease prevention and health education and specifically by providing easy access to confidential healthcare services, promoting sexual health and addressing high risk sexual behaviour – a view shared by Weyman (2003), who identifies a clear role for gynaecology nurses in this context. Berkeley and Ross (2003) argue for a holistic approach to improving the sexual health of young people, involving change at cultural, socio-economic, and service organization levels, something which will require close partnership working and joined-up services.

Nurses are in an ideal position to assume a key role in the collaborative fight to prevent teenage pregnancy, given their presence in local health clinics, general practice surgeries, hospitals, care facilities and schools. As nursing is again reviewing the role of practitioners in the community, healthcare providers with access to new evidence about the consequences of adolescent childbearing may well have a clearer focus on providing competent, successful and compassionate care to pregnant and parenting young people.

Teenage fathers

Teenage fathers

No discussion about pre-teen and teenage pregnancy can be complete without attention being given to teenage fathers. The lives and experiences of teenage fathers have often received less attention from researchers, practitioners and policymakers. As a result of available data on female conception and birth rates, it is often easier to research teenage pregnancy from a purely female perspective. As there is no related data for young fathers, we often know little about teenage fathers and so centre care and support around the pregnant girl and teenage mother. However, there is a growing research interest which now allows a reasonable analysis of the situation for young men (Robinson and Barret, 1982; Springarn and DuRant, 1996; Rhein et al., 1996).

Early age sexual activity and pregnancy

Much of the literature on teenage fathers supports the view that they need just as much support as teenage girls in this situation (Quinlivan and Condon, 2005). Similarly, the need to recognise and support teen fathers is identified by Tyrer *et al.* (2005) who conducted in-depth interviews with young people in local authority care and their carers over four different geographical areas to determine the kinds of support available. Their findings identified social exclusion and inflexible service provision as being problematic issues for the young people concerned. Risk-taking behaviours are also common in both adolescent males and females and are frequently contributing factors to teenage pregnancy. Allen *et al.* (2007) cite socio-economic disadvantage, being born to a teenage mother, drunkenness, drug taking and 'skipping school' as major features leading to teenage pregnancy for both young males and young females in their longitudinal study of thirteen- to sixteen-year-olds covering 27 coeducational secondary schools in central and southern England.

Overall, the literature on teenage fathers identifies the need for improved communication, personal support and development and education as key to reducing the risk of early pregnancy. There is also a significant need for more research related to young fathers, their experiences, support needs and aspirations.

Conclusion

This chapter has highlighted the range and scope of the problem of early age sexual activity and teenage pregnancy. It has presented current data that allows us to take a global, UK and national perspective and covered some of the salient issues that make up the true nature of childhood and adolescence in the twenty-first century. Whilst there is no doubt that a multi-agency approach to this problem is the preferred choice, it is clear that teenage pregnancy poses key challenges for all professionals working with this age group. It is also clear that the training of healthcare professionals and teachers needs to be reconsidered to better prepare them for working with this growing population.

The range and scope of the issues that arise from childhood and teenage pregnancy are broad and problematic. It is the responsibility of all those who engage with young people, whether in a health, education or social work context, to help to tackle them.

Pre-teen and teenage pregnancy

References

Agyei, W.K.A. and Epeme, E.J. (1992) Sexual behaviour and contraceptive use among 15–24 year olds in Uganda. *International Journal of Family Planning Perspectives* **18**: 13–17.

Ajayi, A.A., Marangu, L.T., Miller, J. and Paxman, J.M. (1991) Adolescent sexuality and fertility in Kenya: A survey of knowledge perceptions and practices. *Studies in Family Planning* **22**: 35–41.

Allen, E., Bonnell, C., Strange, A., Copas, A., Stephenson, J., Johnson, A.M. and Oakley, A. (2007) Does the UK government's teenage pregnancy strategy deal with the correct risk factors? Findings from a secondary analysis of data from a randomised trial of sex education and their implications for policy. *Journal of Epidemiology and Community Health* **61**: 20–27.

Allen, J. and Bradley, S. (2001) Family planning provision in the Trent health region: Is it accessible to school age teenagers? *Journal of Family Planning and Reproductive Health Care* **27**(1): 13–15.

Berkeley, D. and Ross, D. (2003) Strategies for improving the sexual health of young people. *Culture, Health and Sexuality* **5**(1): 71–86.

Brennan, K. (2002) *Britain is worst in Europe for teenage pregnancy rates.* Available at http://www.studentbmj.com.

Burford, G. (2006) Families: Their role as architects of civil society and social inclusion. *Practice* **17**(2): 79–88.

Coombes, R. (2002) Sexual healing. *Nursing Times* **98**(24): 10–11.

Crouch, V. (2002) Teenage pregnancy: Better prevention and a sexual health game for young people. *Education and Health* **20**(1): 13–16.

Davey, C. (2005) Sexual and reproductive health and rights in the United Kingdom at ICPD + 10. *Reproductive Health Matters* **13**(25): 81–87.

DH (2000) *The NHS Plan: A plan for investment, a plan for reform.* London: DH.

DH (2001a) *Briefing Paper for Regional Stakeholder Events: Teenage Pregnancy* London: DH.

DH (2001b) *Better Prevention, Better Services, Better Sexual Health – The national strategy for sexual health and HIV.* London: DH.

DH (2006) Abortion statistics, England and Wales: 2005. *Statistical Bulletin* 2006(1) London: DH

Dimond, B. (2002) Legal issues: Teenage pregnancy and the law. *British Journal of Midwifery* **10**(2): 105–108.

Fathalla, M.F. (1994) Women's health: An overview. *International Journal of Gynaecological Obstetrics* **46**: 105–118.

Foote, J. (1997) Practice: Teenage suicide attempts. *Nursing Times* **93**(22): 46–48.

Early age sexual activity and pregnancy

Family Planning Association (2006) *About Us: Locations in the Community.* Available at http://www.fpa.org.uk/community/young people (accessed May 2007)

Fullerton, D. (2005) 'More than Words' – Parents' influence on adolescent sexual health: Findings from a systematic review. In NHS Health Scotland (2005) *Parents – Caught in the crossfire promoting positive sexual wellbeing.* Available at http://www.healthscotland.com (accessed May 2007).

Gorgen, R., Maier, B. and Diesfeld, H.J. (1993) Problems related to schoolgirl pregnancies in Burkina Faso. *Studies in Family Planning* 24: 283–294.

Harner, H.M. (2004) Domestic violence and trauma care in teenage pregnancy: Does parental age make a difference? *Journal of Obstetric, Gynaecologic and Neonatal Nursing* 33(3): 312–319.

Health Protection Agency (2006) *Diagnoses of selected STDs by region, sex and age group United Kingdom: 1996–2005.* London: Health Protection Agency.

Health Protection Scotland (2006) *Weekly Report 42.* Available at http://www.hps.scot.nhs.uk (accessed May 2007).

Herring, J. (1997) Children's abortion rights. *Medical Law Review* 5: 257–268.

HMSO (1998) *The Human Rights Act.* (1998) London: HMSO.

Jackson, E. (2003) *Regulating Reproduction.* Oxford: Hart Publishing.

Johnson, A. (2002) Sexual behaviour in Britain: Partnerships, practices and HIV risk behaviours. *The Lancet* 358: 1835–1842.

Kennedy, J.W., Reinholt, C. and Angelini, P.J. (1997) Ethnic differences in childhood and adolescent sexual abuse and teenage pregnancy. *Journal of Adolescent Health* 21(1): 3–10.

Langer, A. (2002) Unwanted pregnancy: Impact on health and society in Latin America and the Caribbean. *Pan American Journal of Public Health* 11(3): 192–204.

Lee, N. (1999) The challenge of childhood. *Childhood* 6(4): 455–474.

Legge, A. (2002) Playing it safe. *Nursing Times* 98(31): 20–23.

Lesser, J. and Escoto-Lloyd, S. (1999) Health-related problems in a vulnerable population: Pregnant teens and adolescent mothers. *Nursing Clinics of North America* 34(2): 289–299.

Logsdon, M.C. (2004) Depression in adolescent girls: Screening and intervention strategies for primary care providers. *Journal of American Medical Women's Association* 59: 101–106.

Marie Stopes International Organisation (2007) *Young people.* Available at http://www.mariestopes.org.uk/ww/ (accessed May 2007).

McClain, N. (2003) Critical thinking in critical care: Adolescent suicide attempt, undisclosed secrets. *Paediatric Nursing* 29(1): 52–53.

National Statistics (2005) Amendment *Health Statistics Quarterly* 26 & 27 London: National Statistics.

Perry, A. (2002) Teenage pregnancy and the midwife: Exhuming the Social Exclusion Report. *Midwifery Matters* (93): 7–10.

Pre-teen and teenage pregnancy

Pritchard, C. and Mason, T. (2000) Breaking the cycle of disadvantage: Young people, social exclusion and mental health. *Mental Health Care* 4(1): 14–17.

Public Health Institute of Scotland (2000) *Sexual Health in Britain: Recent changes in high risk sexual behaviours and the epidemiology of sexually transmitted infections including HIV.*
Available at http://www.phis.org.uk (accessed May 2007).

Quinlivan, J. A. and Condon, J. (2005) Anxiety and depression in fathers in teenage pregnancy. *Australia and New Zealand Journal of Psychiatry* 39 (10): 915–920.

Rhein, L., Ginsburg, K., Pinto-Martin, J., Swarz, D. and Slap, G. (1996) Teen father participation in childrearing: Family perspectives. *Journal of Adolescent Health* 21(4): 244–252.

Robinson, B. E. and Barret, R. L. (1982) Issues and problems related to the research on teenage fathers: A critical analysis. *Journal of School Health* 52(10): 596–600.

Royal Institute of Public Health (2007) http://www.riph.org.uk
(last accessed May 2007).

Scottish Health Service (1998) *Teenage Pregnancy in Scotland: A 15-Year Review* Edinburgh: Common Services Agency.

Scottish Health Statistics (2006) *Teenage Pregnancy* Office of Information and Statistics Data, NHS National Services Scotland.
Available at http://www.isdscotland.org (accessed May 2007).

Scottish Health Statistics (2007) *ISD National Statistics Release: Abortions by age group 1968–2005.* Available at http://www.isdscotland.org.

Sheldon, S. (1997) *Beyond Control: Medical power and abortion law.* London: Pluto Press.

Singh, S. and Darroch, J.E. (2000) Adolescent pregnancy and childbearing: Levels and trends in developed countries. *International Journal of Family Planning Perspectives* 32: 14–23.

Smith, J. (1997) Promoting the sexual health of young people: Part 1. *Paediatric Nursing* 9(2): 24–27.

Social Exclusion Unit (1999) *Teenage Pregnancy.* London: DH.

Springarn, R.W. and DuRant, R.H. (1996) Male adolescents involved in pregnancy: Associated health risk and problem behaviours. *Journal of Adolescent Health* 18: 121–127.

Sutton, H. (2001) Sexual health promotion: Reducing the rate of teenage pregnancy. *Journal of Paediatric Nursing* 13(3): 33–37.

The Stationery Office (2000) *Sexual Offences Amendment Act (2000).* London: The Stationery Office.

Turner, R.J., Sorenson, A.M. and Turner, J.B. (2000) Social contingencies in mental health: A seven year follow up study of teenage mothers. *Journal of Marriage and Family* 62(3): 777–791.

Early age sexual activity and pregnancy

Tyrer, P., Chase, E., Warwick, I. and Aggelton, P. (2005) 'Dealing with It': Experiences of young fathers in and leaving care. *British Journal of Social Work* 35(7): 1107–1121.

UNICEF (1998) *The Progress of Nations.* Geneva: UNICEF.

Wellings, K. (2001) Sexual Behaviour in Britain: Early heterosexual experience. *The Lancet* **358**: 1346–1351.

Wellings, K. and Field, B. (1996) Sexual behaviour and young people. *Clinical Obstetrics and Gynaecology* **10**(1): 139–160.

Weyman, A. (2003) Promoting sexual health to young people: Preventing teenage pregnancy and sexually transmitted infections. *Journal of the Royal Society for the Promotion of Health* **123**(1): 66–69.

Whitehead, E. (2001) Teenage pregnancy: On the road to social death. *International Journal of Nursing Studies* 38(4): 437–444.

WHO (2004) *Adolescent Pregnancy Issues in Adolescent Health and Development.* Geneva: WHO.

WHO (2006) *Pregnant Adolescents: Delivering on global promises of hope.* Geneva: WHO.

Chapter 3
A child of our time
James Moir

The study of childhood has been mainly limited in social sciences to the study of cognitive and emotional development in psychology, and the processes of institutional socialisation in sociology. Much this work has considered the way in which children pass through stages on their way to maturity as adults. Both approaches have examined how children learn and develop through interaction with adults and, as such, how their visibility as a distinct social category has become a matter to be attended to.

This chapter outlines the development, not of the child, but rather the concept of 'child'. In other words, it takes a step back to consider what we understand a child to be and how the adult-child relationship is translated into expectations about how adults communicate with children and vice versa. This is important given that what children are expected to know about and act upon is shifting discourse over time, and nowhere is this more contentious and sharply focused than in the area of sex and relationships education. Talking about sex within the context of the expectations surrounding the adult-child dichotomy has never been easy, but now there is an expectation that children should be encouraged to express their views and evidence their evolving 'maturity' with respect to these 'adult' issues. This is of great significance for sex education given the fundamental role of communication in this field. However, first the story of the 'child of our time' has to be told. It is a story of how children are now both seen and heard.

According to Aries' classic 1965 book – *Centuries of Childhood* – the notion of childhood did not even exist in medieval society and children, as a distinct social category, were therefore 'invisible'. The 'child' in effect became part of the adult world soon after infancy with no attempt to delineate age or physical maturity. More recently, Pollock has contested this claim that the status of childhood did not emerge until the seventeenth century and denies that children were simply integrated into adult life (Pollock, 1983). Jenks offers a third interpretation, demonstrating that the western concept of childhood is culture-specific and continues to evolve over time (Jenks, 1996). For example, Rousseau's novel *Emile*, published in the early nineteenth century, presents an image of childhood which prefigures modern developmental psychology. He argues that this period of life involves a distinct way of perceiving, thinking and feeling and that this unfolding maturational process is open to corruption by societal influences and, in particular, through interactions with adults. We see the vestiges of this view of childhood today, where childhood is regarded as a natural state and stage of being which must be protected from corruption.

This modern view developed in parallel with the advent of child-centred urban domestic families in western Europe from the end of the eighteenth century. The focus moved to the nature of the relationship between parents and children, although in Victorian Britain this was often encapsulated in the idiomatic phrase that 'children should be seen and not heard'. This moral prescription that children should be quiet and kept from intruding into the adult world did, in effect, demarcate a world of childhood within the conscious practice of family life. This was then reinforced through the separation of the child from work and the provision of state education.

By the mid-twentieth century, childhood had become a distinct stage of life associated with the notion of moral and psychological development and a burgeoning child-rearing and family advice literature soon followed. This literature, of both academic and populist books and articles, has promoted a discourse built around the 'needs' of the child. Much of it prescribes the means by which these needs can be met to allow children to grow and thrive, as if part of a natural aspect of the life cycle. Many of the ideas have their roots in developmental psychology, and in particular the work of Piaget, who identified stages of intellectual growth, with each new stage developing out of, and incorporating, the previous one.

Modern and post-modern views of childhood

Views of childhood

Jenks (1996) regards Piaget's age-and-stage approach as in keeping with the modern view in which the child only comes to know the adult world in a gradual manner. Childhood is therefore accorded considerable weight in terms of the total life experience and adults need to attend to children's developing cognitive and affective development. He also points out that childhood has become associated with material provision, which is taken to be natural and grounded in an ideology of care guided by emotional discourse.

We have a culture in which adults are expected to act in the child's interests and this legitimates the large amount of economic and cultural capital invested in the promise of childhood. Jenks calls this 'futurity' – a discourse of caring for, enabling and facilitating children to become morally well-adjusted adults. In the modern world, children are encouraged to be more visible and to be heard (rather than seen and not heard) and this has become enshrined in UK law, in the form of the 1989 Children Act which provides children with a number of rights, the principal among which is the right to have their views taken into account.

In the post-modern age, Jenks then sees mass education and patterns of consumption as having shortened childhood and undermined it. It is increasingly difficult for children to build a sense of identity as part of a reflexive self. The lines of demarcation between adults and children have become blurred and the normative markers of status between the two have been transformed. According to Jenks, we now have a variety of lifestyles and associated child-rearing practices which are relativised through the media. By contrast, Mayall believes that childhood identities can be associated with moral agency and there may be greater scope for the interpretation and negotiation of this in the home than at school (Mayall, 2002).

Whatever the case, children are increasingly heard. They learn to speak and negotiate their way through childhood by adopting certain ways of talking, aided in this by an adult world that encourages them to adopt a particular discourse of accounting for their actions through psychological 'explanations'. It is through this way of talking that children learn to become accountable moral agents in the world, expected to express 'thoughts', 'opinions', 'views' and 'feelings'. We live in an age of discourse within a discourse of age in which children are actively encouraged to be consulted and to speak on a number of issues that would have previously been the preserve of the adult world.

Talking children

Talking children

One of the most important things that children must learn is to make themselves 'visible' as agents of and in the world. Perhaps one of the key aspects of childhood today is the extent to which children are part of the age of discourse. This can be characterised in two ways: firstly as a feature of the post-modern concern with 'communication' and secondly in terms of Jenks' point about the erosion of the boundary between adulthood and childhood when it comes to self-expression. Children are expected to have their say, to be consulted and to be heard. However, they have to be guided in this by adults to produce the kinds of psychological discourse required. This is often accomplished through prompting children to produce useful opinions, views, and decisions, often aided by various educational and welfare agencies and media campaigns encouraging adults to consult and listen to children.

However, according to Jenks' analysis of childhood in a post-modern age, childhood has now become problematised in terms of its collapsed age range and changed form. There is a concern that childhood is under attack, that it is being lost and that children are no longer able to engage in the practice of being a child for any extended period of life. Childhood has therefore become a site for discourses concerning issues of stability, integration and social bonds (Hunt, 2005). Much of this is focused around the view that children need to acquire conversational skills, that adults need to talk to them more and that children need to be 'free' of commercial pressures to allow them simply to be children. There is a concern that children's psychological growth is being stunted by the lack of an extended period of childhood and, in particular, the lack of interaction and conversational opportunities. Nowhere is this more apparent than in recent press reports. Take the following extract from a recent article in the *Daily Telegraph*.

Extract from the *Daily Telegraph*

Junk culture 'is poisoning our children'

Ben Fenton (12 September 2006)

A sinister cocktail of junk food, marketing, over-competitive schooling and electronic entertainment is poisoning childhood, a powerful lobby of academics and children's experts says today.

In a letter to the *Daily Telegraph*, 110 teachers, psychologists, children's authors and other experts call on the Government to act to prevent the death of childhood. The group, which includes Philip Pullman, the children's author, Jacqueline Wilson, the Children's Laureate, her predecessor Michael Morpurgo, Baroness Greenfield, the director of the Royal Institution, and Dr Penelope Leach, the child care expert, blames a failure by politicians and public alike to understand how children develop.

'Since children's brains are still developing, they cannot adjust...to the effects of ever more rapid technological and cultural change,' they write. They still need what developing human beings have always needed, including real food (as opposed to processed 'junk'), real play (as opposed to sedentary, screen-based entertainment), first-hand experience of the world they live in and regular interaction with the real-life significant adults in their lives. They also need time. In a fast-moving, hyper-competitive culture, today's children are expected to cope with an ever-earlier start to formal schoolwork and an overly academic test-driven primary curriculum. 'They are pushed by market forces to act and dress like mini-adults and exposed via the electronic media to material which would have been considered unsuitable for children even in the very recent past.'

Note the references to maturation as an unfolding process that requires a time of its own and that is enriched through adult-child interaction as well as play and first-hand experience. The underlying concern is a fear of stunted or even damaged cognitive and emotional growth and the need to recover a sense of childhood as a stage towards well-adjusted development.

These concerns have been raised repeatedly over recent years and have led to calls for a greater focus on 'communication skills'. It is suggested that parents need to talk more with their children and that children need to talk more in the school setting. The following two BBC News reports give a flavour of this discussion.

Parents urged to talk to children

3 April 2006

Too much television and a lack of family meals are damaging children's conversational ability, a report says.

The Basic Skills Agency found many parents did not 'see the point' of developing verbal skills, focusing instead on reading and writing. Some four-year-olds threw tantrums in class because they could not communicate in any other way. The BSA wants primary school teachers to work with families to improve children's conversation.

Family 'splintering'

Its report – *Talk to Me* – says verbal skills are declining 'year on year'. It says all-day television, parents' long working hours and the 'decline of the family meal' are causes of poor communication. It also cites the 'splintering' of families into different rooms in the house, with children as young as four watching TV alone in their bedrooms. The 'greatest impact' on children's verbal skills was among disadvantaged families. The report backs US research conducted in the mid-1990s, which found that by the time they started school a child of professional parents had heard about 50 million words. For those of working-class background it was 30 million and for those with parents on income support it was 12 million.

Primary school pupils are to be taught how to speak and listen to each other

4 November 2003

Young children, more used to watching television than talking, are to be encouraged to improve their communication skills.

From next week, every primary school in England will be sent guidance on how to get children to hold discussions and listen to one another. The curriculum watchdog, the Qualifications and Curriculum Authority (QCA), says improving oral skills has a 'key role' in raising standards. Supporting the 'Speaking, Listening, Learning' initiative will be a pack of teaching materials, including a training video for teachers. These materials, which show teachers how to encourage children to improve their speech, are being claimed as the 'first of their kind to be developed anywhere in the world'.

Poor communication skills

There have been concerns that children, who have spent too long watching television and too little time talking to their parents, have arrived at school with poor communication skills. A report from school inspectors from Ofsted recently claimed that too many children beginning school lacked basic social skills and could not even dress themselves. Headteachers had claimed that the behavioural and verbal skills of children starting school were at an all-time low, with some five-year-olds unable to speak properly. This project, from the Primary National Strategy, has the aim of improving children's learning and social skills by helping them to talk to each other and in groups.

These reports highlight the concerns over the 'problem' of children's communication skills in relation to learning and moral development. Again the underlying issue of the need to recover childhood is ever-present.

The moral value afforded to communication is clear: enabling children to talk is beneficial as means of psychological development and for citizenship. This treats self-expression as a positive outcome of development, one in which the children are able to move towards being responsible for themselves and able to display confidence in their capacity for being agents in the world. The practice of childhood in this view is therefore very much in keeping with Mead's notion of a developing sense of self, whilst there is also a concern with cognitive development akin to the Piagetian notion that play and direct experience are crucial to learning.

Childhood as psychological 'development' is therefore very much in evidence in contemporary discussions and debates. In this view, learning to converse is linked to the idea that talk functions as a forward-referenced means of moving the child along towards adulthood. The way children talk is therefore treated as an index of the developmental stage they are at, both in terms of cognition and moral development.

As Edwards (1997) points out with respect to infant cognition, this is largely a *post hoc* enterprise with an idealised model of adult cognition as the 'end point' and a linear path drawn towards how the child reaches this point. The presence or absence of some form of reasoning is taken as indicating how far along the developmental path the child has travelled. Much the same kind of argument can be made with respect to children's conversational skills. These are often taken as 'language development' because of what comes later. How children talk is read across to expectations for their age to determine how far they have advanced along the adult-child continuum of conversational competency. If a child appears too far ahead for their age then they are seen as precocious; too far behind and they may be regarded as out of step and immature.

The 'socialisation problem'

Socialisation problem

Edwards also points out that the learnability of discursive and other cultural practices follows from their visibility and public nature. In other words, children learn ways of talking, a psychological discourse that can be acquired, through participation in public practices. Sacks (1972, 1992) referred to this as the 'socialisation problem' – the way in which new members learn to take part in virtue of taking part. Children learn how to project their agency and competency towards becoming an adult through the adoption of this kind of discourse.

Sacks considered this as a designed-to-be-acquirable 'visible' feature of conversational competence such that the vocabularies of motive could be utilised and subverted. He notes that accountable actions can either be characterised as results of inevitable direct causation or, more loosely and indirectly, associated with another action. Parents can subvert the indirect association by turning it into a matter of direct causation (for example, a punishment that inevitably follows a misdemeanour by the child). Sacks also observes that children can learn which aspects of their behaviour are seen as evidence for their 'prior intention' and actions, and subvert this process by producing such behaviour deliberately to confirm adults' assumptions. Thus the inferential visibility of moral conduct is something that children learn in terms of seeing matters and talking about them.

This is a very different treatment of socialisation from Mead's (1934) account and later refinements by Denzin (1977) and Shibutani (1955). In these accounts of socialisation, children acquire a sense of self through interactions with significant others and pass through various stages on their way to becoming a person-in-society. For Mead this involves three stages that culminate in the child's ability to learn the expectations and moral prescriptions bound up with the various roles they play in society. The later refinements by Denzin and Shibutani consider issues of interactional age and reference groups respectively in this process. However, despite these modifications, there is still the tendency to consider socialisation as a process in which children acquire a distinct psychological sense of self and this has become the core 'problem' to be examined.

Even sociologists with a more direct connection with sociolinguistics, such as Bourdieu (1977, 1992), posit such a view by referring to a theorisation of *habitus* that trades on an unreflexive cognitivist account of development. This presupposes the development of a psychological system in which dispositions associated with membership of social and cultural groups come to generate practices, perceptions and attitudes. This system is then able to produce 'meaning' from these (that is, make sense of them) and then store and process it. Whilst Bourdieu gives more weight to sociolinguistic practices and culture, he cannot rid himself of this 'inner/outer' dualism and the reification of the child developing as a person in terms of a 'mind' that functions as a perceptual system. The point here is that the 'problem' is reduced to one of a theory of mind rather than an examination of sociolinguistic practices and how these are learned as practices.

Heritage (1991) has drawn attention to the way in which social actors during conversation treat one another as agents, based on the assumption that talk is under voluntary control and that what is said is treated as morally accountable. These cultural-discursive practices are a feature of childhood that is learnable by virtue of this engagement in discursive psychology. These psychological representations provide the means for a varied way of engaging in social and institutional life and a means of making it intelligible and orderly. Cognitive references to 'thinking', giving 'reasons', 'knowing' 'interpreting' or 'understanding' provide publicly accountable criteria for agency and set operational moves that can be applied as a resource for agency and its accountability. Take, for example, the references to 'thinking things through' or 'thinking before acting'. These are yardsticks for agency with respect to various discursive activities such as making 'decisions' and how far children are along the adult-child continuum in terms of their maturity of thought.

Cognition is regarded as the element of control that provides a basis for thinking before acting. The affective or emotional element is being taken as spontaneous and representing 'feelings' that nonetheless can be taken to account for action within conversation. The emotional basis for action, or indeed inaction, can be presented as understandable, as a means for literally moving a person to do, or not do, something. It is often portrayed as an influence on how people think, where thinking is reasoning and emotion is a means of supporting, skewing or bypassing the reasoning process. Reason implies stability and order in how people conduct themselves; unchecked emotion can therefore be seen as threatening or dangerous.

This duality is interesting in terms of the ways in which the discursive usage of emotion terms can be a flexible and useful means of characterising action. Again, the sophistication with which children are able to deploy them in practice is taken as indicating how developed they are as human beings. As Edwards (1997) notes, emotional discourse can be put to a great variety of uses within a range of social practices:

- emotional terms can be contrasted with cognitions in terms of their less deliberative nature
- emotional terms can be taken as being as 'understandable' and appropriate – how any 'reasonable' person would react
- emotional terms can be characterised as being the outcome of events or in the nature of the person
- emotional terms can be treated as being kept under the control of a person's reasoning or reactions that resist control; and
- emotional terms can be presented as the interaction of mental and physiological systems, as natural, or as derived from moral and ethical concerns.

The 'socialisation problem' here is how children learn these sorts of contrasting ways of using 'emotion talk' across a range of social practices and their normative associations. Studying how children deploy these ways of talking, either in terms of direct psychological accounting, or in terms of orientation towards aspects of an inner/outer dualism, can aid exploration of their socialisation into a usage of a major cultural dualism: taking people's 'outward' accounts and actions and considering these as representations of what they are like 'inside' as thinking and feeling agents. I want to stress that this derives from accountability within conversational practices rather than as the result of some sort of inner mental cognitive processing and exchange of representations between interlocutors.

The prevailing cognitivist view

Cognitivist view

A perceptual-cognitivist view of people's actions is the basis of much psychological investigation which trades on the assumption that people are concerned with interacting with one another in order to understand what they are thinking and feeling. This is part of a wider cultural commonplace, an 'inner/outer' dualism, which is integral to a range of social practices. The notion of these two separate realms is therefore a major rhetorical feature that is incorporated into how people engage with one another in conversation. It provides a means of trading notions of 'sense making' as well as the portrayal of people's 'inner' mental states. There is a huge cultural imperative to be able to talk in terms of one's 'thoughts' and 'feelings' in the form of judgements, reasons and evaluations, as the outcome of some kind of mental process. In perceptual-cognitive processing terms it is an 'input-process-output' model.

Children therefore need to learn how to 'talk the psychological talk' as part of the social practices that they engage in, and they learn this by interaction with adults and other children. It is something that is orientated towards conversation in terms of how they portray individual attitudes, beliefs, motives, goals, judgements and so on. Notice here that orientating to something does not necessarily involve an explicit mention of these psychological terms but rather the way in which people treat one another as if attitudes, beliefs, motives and so on are germane or at stake. In effect, this orientation is one of a conversational set of discourses that refer to an intra-psychic world. This is something that is normatively attended to as a means of accomplishing order within conversation. It is this that children learn – ways of talking as a means of accomplishing actions in the world.

This cultural-discursive practice is founded upon an orientation of interlocutors as employing a discourse of mental processes in order to account for how they perceive matters and how they and others act. Events are prior to this operation. They have happened and need to be communicated, to be 'understood' in terms of emotional response. In this model there is a realm of people placed in amongst events and occurrences and a realm of mental operations requiring to be brought together.

Here, rationality is associated with the psychological notion of 'perception'. Accounts of, and about, actions are presented as part of texts of 'meaning' in which a mental processing system is assumed to be brought to bear upon matters in order to display these as the result of psychological agents who reach 'decisions', have feelings, have deliberated on something or other or who can account for something in a way that 'makes sense' to others who can understand a course of action. It is interesting to note here how even 'emotion talk' as the basis for actions may nonetheless be treated as rational in terms of their accountability or intelligibility. We can see why a person might act in a particular way given the way that they react to certain circumstances.

This view sees 'development' as going beyond the acquisition of socio-linguistic skills to learning how discourse works in all its contrastive and flexible ways as a means for accomplishing action. It is not that children learn the notion of 'causation' for example and can understand what it means as a way of 'making sense'. Rather it is, as Edwards (1997) tellingly points out, that it is a discursive means for explanation as something that is required precisely because there are other sorts of discourse that can be deployed contrastively against it: intentions, reasons, coincidences, mistakes and so on. The availability of different sorts of explanations is what makes explanation such a key resource for children to learn to use.

Beyond cognitivist assumptions

As noted above, psychological investigation typically trades on a 'sense making' rhetoric in which the mind is theorised as a mental system that operates upon an external reality in order to produce a rational account of it. The aim of cognitive psychology is to examine, usually via experiments, how this system 'works'. The assumption is made that there are two realms: an external reality which acts as 'raw material' and 'input' for a psychological system which then operates on this input in some way to produce an 'output' such as a perception. The de-coupling of cognitive activity from social practice, and particularly through little or no reference to everyday conversation, is what makes this activity easier to portray as cognitive development.

If we eschew these notions of cognitive and emotional development, we can consider child socialisation instead in terms of the management of the discourse of the relationship between 'mind' and 'reality'. This is not for the child some developmental issue to be resolved so as to reach adult competence but rather a practical sociological construction within conversation that they must learn. Much has been written recently about the discursive means by which people construct such an association (Edwards & Potter, 1992; Edwards, 1997; Potter 1996 and 2003; Molder &

Potter, 2005) but there is much less of a discussion as to how children learn to deploy discursive psychology. This is what I wish to concentrate upon in the remainder of this chapter. In doing so I wish to focus upon these rhetorical constructions in which the use of a perceptual rhetoric is associated with a mental world of knowing and understanding. This is a key feature of adult-child interaction because it is considered to be central to the notion of development. Adults can gauge a child's level of understanding in terms of how they see matters. That is how children make their thinking, and hence themselves, visible.

Both sets of practices are fundamental to the way children learn to present themselves as agents in the world and are treated as such by adults within conversation. Again it is worth reiterating at this point that my focus here is on the construction of conversational practices in making use of this culturally embedded inner/outer dualism, rather than taking this as read.

Learning to present an 'inner' psychology

An 'inner' psychology

A major part of a child's everyday engagement in conversational practices at home and at school involves showing 'understanding'. Indeed, because childhood is taken as being an unprecedented period of learning, then children are expected to demonstrate their learning as a sign of development. Children need to learn to present themselves as psychological agents in terms of 'mental processes' being required to operate upon an external world in order to 'make sense' of it. In this way the events are placed prior to this operation, as having happened and needing to be 'understood'. Talking about 'making sense' of matters is a kind of grammar that allows interlocutors to stabilise versions of events. Indeed, to refer to matters as 'nonsense' or 'making no sense' is part of this process; a discourse that stabilises matters in the routine of the conversation.

In this model, there is a realm of events and occurrences and a realm of mental operations that have to be brought together in order for us to apprehend or grasp the nature of these events and occurrences. In this way the selection and active constitution of these matters as a social practice is occluded through the reification of 'reality' and 'mind', through the 'external' world that requires to be 'understood' or 'made sense' of by an inner mental processing system that 'perceives' that outer reality. It is a discourse that children learn, often through parental and teacher checks upon their 'understanding'.

This association between the presentation of objects, events and occurrences and the mental operations that have been applied to them provides a means of establishing rationality as inhering in the child as an agent and as a measure of their development. In this way a perceptual-cognitivist form of conversational practice is actively maintained through an inner/outer dualism in which the child is encouraged to look out onto the world in order to 'make sense' of it. This outer world presents itself as requiring 'interpretation' or 'understanding' in terms of an active 'inner' response. It can also be the basis for creating a version of temporality in which what 'has happened' is taken as apparent in how children learn to account for 'decisions' or 'choices'.

Actions are manufactured in the course of practices that require such accounting. There is a huge cultural imperative to produce in conversation, or at least attempt to produce in conversation, normatively appropriate psychological discourse that fits with particular social relations and interactions. For example, children learn that references to 'thinking' are taken as indications of deliberation and intent whilst references to 'feelings' can be used to portray actions as arising out of spontaneously being gripped by emotion.

Children therefore learn that the basis for agency has to be publicly intelligible and their accounts must attend to this. In this sense, the hearer of such an account is positioned 'outside' a child's 'thinking' as another but external psychological agent who must, in the course of the account, employ his or her own inner processes in order to know the other's mind. Perhaps this is what makes dialogue such a powerful means of helping children learn to produce accounts of themselves as psychological agents. They have to learn that dialogue is predicated upon the construction of talk based upon the maintenance of a perceptual-cognitive discourse and the notion that unless we account for our actions through this discourse those actions will be taken as, literally, non-sense. Socialisation here is learning how to display 'understandings', 'interpretations' or 'feelings'.

Conclusions

The notion of these two separate realms – inner mind and external matters that interact – is therefore a major rhetorical feature that children learn in order to portray themselves in conversation as psychological agents. It provides a means of trading on notions of 'sense making' and social order as well as the portrayal of 'inner' mental states and processes as related to their actions.

This is a different notion of socialisation and the value of conversation than that driving the present claims concerning the crisis in childhood. Perhaps it is because our culture has placed so much emphasis upon the notion of the psychological individual that there is such an interest in getting children to talk more, rather than because children are currently mute because they watch too much television or play too many computer games.

Parents and teachers are certainly now being encouraged to invest more time and effort in talking to children. This is put down to encouraging child development in terms of learning ability and moral development. Toward the end of primary school and into secondary school such matters include sex education and, in many cases, the problem of teenage pregnancy. However, the danger of such an approach is that it becomes confined to the discourse of education, something that children may regard as being foisted upon them as part of an over-arching moral concern about the corruption of childhood to encourage development towards responsible adulthood.

I have sought to provide an alternative account of child 'development'. It is one that is based on how children acquire the ability to use language as a means to accomplish actions as an adult competence through their immersion in cultural-discursive practices. It is more than mere acquisition of social skills but rather the ability to use discourse as a public and visible means of engaging in the world. This is a crucial point when it comes to encouraging children to take part in moral discussions concerning sexual relations, given that such discussions deal with the very language through which these relations are negotiated and managed.

It is this broader context that perhaps needs to inform sex education in order to prevent it from becoming a 'topic' for discussion in school and with parents. By grounding such discussions within a reflexive examination of discourses, childhood, morality and development, it may be possible to open up sex education to a more 'critical' examination by children of the way they are located within cultural-discursive practices. I do not wish to suggest for one moment that children should or could become reflexive sociologists but rather that sex education should be made relevant to contemporary children. To do otherwise is to treat sex education and the issue of teenage pregnancy in a decontextualised fashion, making it a narrow topic for discussion instead of part of a wider discussion of contradictory and competing views of the status of children maturing towards adulthood in the modern world.

References

Aries, P. (1965) *Centuries of Childhood* London: Cape.

Bourdieu, P. (1977) *Outline of a Theory of Practice* Cambridge: Cambridge University Press.

Bourdieu, P. (1992) *Language and Symbolic Powe.* Polity Press: London.

Denzin, N. (1977) *Childhood Socialisatio.* San Francisco: Jossey-Bass.

Edwards, D. (1997) *Discourse and Cognition* London: Sage.

Edwards, D. and Potter, J. (1992) *Discursive Psychology* London: Sage.

Heritage, J. Intention, meaning and strategy: observations on constraints in interaction analysis. *Research on Language in Social Interaction* 24: 311–32.

Hunt, S. (2005) *The Life Course* Basingstoke: Palgrave MacMillan.

Jenks, C. (1996) *Childhood* London: Routledge.

Mayall, B. (2002) *Towards a Sociology of Childhood* Oxford: Oxford University Press.

Mead, G.H. (1934) *Mind, Self and Society* Berkeley: University of California Press.

Molder, H. and Potter, J (eds.) (2005) *Conversation and Cognition* Cambridge: Cambridge University Press.

Pollock, L. (1983) *Forgotten Children.* Cambridge: Cambridge University Press.

Potter, J. (1996) *Representing Reality: Discourse rhetoric and social construction* London: Sage.

Potter, J. (2003) Discursive Psychology: Between method and paradigm. *Discourse and Society* 14(6): 783–794.

Sacks, H. (1972) Notes on police assessment of moral character. In D.N. Sudnow (ed.) *Studies in Social Interaction* New York: Free Press.

Sacks, H. (1992) *Lectures on Conversation I and II* Jefferson, G. (ed.) Oxford: Blackwell Scientific Press.

Shibutani, T. (1955) Reference groups as perspectives. *American Journal of Sociology* 60: 562–569.

Chapter 4
Adolescent risk taking in sexual behaviours
Theo Kwansa

Risky sexual behaviours among young people have, over the years, become a national and international concern. The prevalence and increasing incidence of sexually transmitted diseases (STDs), particularly among young people, and the high incidence of unintended and unplanned pregnancies have led to extensive public debates, research and national initiatives within the UK and other countries. In the UK, the National Strategy for Sexual Health and HIV and the Sexual Health Strategy for Scotland aim to minimise the multiple health consequences and irreparable damage that may be caused by certain forms of STDs. An equally important aim is to reduce the incidence of adolescent conceptions and early parenthood among young people. Therefore, true 'sexual health' is vital if these and their associated problems are to be eliminated. The World Health Organisation (WHO) defines sexual health as:

> A state of physical, emotional, mental and social wellbeing related to sexuality; it is not merely the absence of disease, dysfunction or infirmity. Sexual health requires a positive and respectful approach to sexuality and sexual relationships, as well as the possibility of having pleasurable and safe sexual experiences, free of coercion, discrimination and violence. For sexual health to be attained and maintained, the sexual rights of all persons must be respected, protected and fulfilled.
>
> (WHO, 2002)

This chapter examines the influencing factors and potential impact – physical, psychological and social consequences – associated with early sexual activity. The role and potential benefits of sexual health education and other community strategies are also explored to outline the range of collaborative approaches that can be employed to meet the complex challenges of teenage sexual risk behaviours.

Sexuality and sex: uncertainties of the adolescent period

Sexuality and sex

While 'sexuality' generally refers to interest in sexual activity, 'sex' generally refers to actual engagement in, or the act of, sexual activity (Sutherland, 2005). In its broader sense, however, sexuality should be seen as encompassing the expression of sexual characteristics – the physical, mental, psychological and emotional traits, including gender identity and sexual orientation (the inherent sexual attraction to the opposite, same or both sexes). The adolescent period of transition from childhood to adulthood involves complex processes of development which invariably affect an individual's perceptions, behaviours, attitudes and the way he or she reacts to different situations and experiences.

A time of trepidation

The complex hormonal influences relating to an adolescent's development of the secondary sex characteristics also arouse more awareness in their sexuality and an interest in sex. Girls generally develop and demonstrate their sexual awareness and sexual attraction earlier than boys. That awareness of sexuality is often accompanied by some degree of anxiety (Sutherland, 2005).

The hormonally-regulated sexual and physical development – puberty – in the adolescent boy involves complex interactions of the androgen hormones from the pituitary, the testes and the adrenals. This pubertal development is characterised by appearance of the secondary sex characteristics, in particular growth of the penis, enlargement of the larynx with deepening of the voice and facial and body hair growth at the armpits and pubic area. These are accompanied by acceleration of growth in height and weight – mainly muscle bulk (Brook, 1981). A characteristic increase in sweat gland activity that also occurs at this time may result in onset of acne of varying degrees of severity (Huebner, 2000).

The young adolescent female's pubertal development is also hormonally regulated by the complex interactions of pituitary and ovarian hormones. The distinctive secondary sex characteristics in this case include the onset of the menstrual cycle – the menarche – and enlargement of the breasts. While there is a notable associated increase in physical growth and weight gain, in this case the weight is attributable to increased fat deposits (Huebner, 2000).

Impact of the pubertal and physical changes

Impact of physical changes

In most adolescents this period of sexual and physical changes is also accompanied by complex development of personality, sexual identity and various psychological manifestations (Steinberg and Morris, 2001). The psychological impact may depend on the extent of these changes and an individual's perceptions and reaction to what they are experiencing at the time. These vary from one person to another. While some degree of clumsiness may accompany the accelerated growth in the young adolescent boy, the adolescent girl is more likely to demonstrate self-consciousness and emotional sensitivity.

Factors influencing the pubertal reactions and perceptions

Influencing factors

For many adolescents the development of the secondary sex characteristics heralds a transition from childhood to the beginning of adulthood which could cause them considerable apprehension and nervousness (Brooks, 1981). The personal, social and cultural basis of an adolescent's sexual anxieties include the nature of relationships to which the individual has been exposed. The impact of relationships dominated by violence, coercion and fear could be loss of self-confidence and confusion about their own sexuality. Various factors contribute to these personal anxieties and may be associated with:

- the family values and principles,
- the nature of relationships within the family, for example:
  - mother-daughter relationship and the young adolescent girl's perception of her mother as the role model of her femininity
  - the father-son relationship and the young adolescent boy's perception of his father as the role model of his transition to manhood.
  - the young adolescent person's relationships with their siblings.
- cultural values and beliefs as well as the religious principles that have guided their upbringing

● peer values, beliefs and principles, and

● conflicting messages conveyed in the media's portrayal of gender, sexuality and sex (Hermiston, 2004).

The young adolescent's self-image in relation to their physical changes could intensify their concerns and apprehensions. The adolescent girl's concerns may be linked to the overall change in her body shape, while the rate and extent of enlargement of her breasts and the onset of menstruation may cause additional apprehension or even distress for some young girls. The adolescent boy's concerns may be linked to the changes in his sex organs, physical stature, his voice and body hair growth, which could cause some degree of clumsiness and nervousness. In some adolescents rather severe acne may have a damaging effect on their self-image and self-confidence (Sutherland, 2005). Another source of trepidation is the taunting, bullying and humiliation that individuals may have to endure relating to differences in the development of their secondary sex characteristics and manifestation of their sexuality.

Adolescent sexuality and related implications

Adolescent sexuality

The period of adolescence seems to be eclipsed by those aspects of human development considered as sexuality. While adolescent girls tend to demonstrate their sexual identity and interest in sex earlier and in more overt ways than boys, the experience of sexual needs and related anxieties ought to be seen as a common phenomenon among both groups. Nonetheless, a notable gender difference in the way these issues are addressed is the degree of emphasis that is usually placed on adolescent females. This is because of the sexual risk outcomes of pregnancy, early parenthood, abortions and possible life-threatening complications. On the theme of 'Reducing the Rate of Teenage Pregnancies', the Health Education Authority published five factual documents in 1999.

● *The Implications of Research into Young People, Sex, Sexuality and Relationships*
   This document provided a review of the existing knowledge about young people's sexuality, their relationships and sexual behaviours, how they prioritised these and how they talked

about sex. The information obtained could serve as a guide to the development of effective programmes for reducing underage pregnancies. The document also outlines recommendations for policy and practice (Aggleton *et al.*, 1998).

● *An Overview of the Effectiveness of Interventions and Programmes Aimed at Reducing Unintended Conceptions in Young People*
This document highlighted the key elements of effective programmes and interventions that were being implemented to reduce the risk of early teenage unintended and unwanted pregnancies (Meyrick and Swann, 1999).

● *Young People's Experiences of Relationships, Sex, and Early Parenthood: Qualitative research*
The findings from this study provided insight into the factors that influence teen sexual behaviours. Their perceptions and attitudes towards pregnancy and parenthood in adolescent years were also explored in relation to situations such as being in local authority care, truanting and expulsion from school (Hughes, 1999).

● *An International Review of Evidence: Data from Europe*
This document presented the trends in teenage conceptions, births and abortions rates in European countries. Of particular importance to professional practice is that it also highlighted the factors that influence the differences in the incidence of these between those European countries (Kane and Wellings, 1999).

● *An International Review of Evidence: US, Canada, Australia, and New Zealand*
This document examined the factors that influenced adolescent conceptions in those countries. It also drew attention to specific lessons that could be learned from the related policies and practices (Cheesbrough *et al.*, 1999).

It is clearly evident from the issues addressed in the above documents that the problem of sexual risk behaviours among young people is a serious concern and a national priority. However, if these problems are to be addressed effectively then it is vital to talk to young people to gain their perspective on them. This will enable service providers and policymakers to gain deeper insight and understanding of the perceptions, sexual behaviours and attitudes of young people towards pregnancy and early parenthood.

Pre-teen and teenage pregnancy

Hughes' (1999) report reveals that strategies used to engage young people to reflect on their life opportunities, their lived experiences and to articulate their perceptions and views do provide the right kind of information for examining, critically, their unique concerns and attitudes to specific issues. This approach can provide a rich resource of information and a clear picture of young people's perspectives on:

- pregnancy
- early parenthood and the impact on their lives
- their relationships
- sex
- contraception and family planning services
- sexual health education and
- the proposed policies about reducing teenage pregnancy rates.

The significance of social deprivation, poverty and low socio-economic status as key contributors to high pregnancy rates among adolescents and young adults cannot be trivialised. Research evidence may have helped to raise awareness of the strategies employed by the Department of Health to reduce teenage conception rates. Nevertheless, public debates still continue to challenge how consistently, how effectively and how successfully those initiatives have been achieved. Commenting on an earlier intention by the Government to reduce the incidence of morbidity among young people relating to high incidence of smoking and unwanted pregnancies, Jacobson and Wilkinson (1994) noted that there was no reliable and consistent policy or efficient procedure at the time for achieving the envisaged improvements. Clearly, there should be a direct link between teenage concerns and views and all the initiatives, policies and procedures designed to improve young people's sexual risk behaviours and related consequences. Equally importantly, the underlying problems and contributing factors need to be explored, carefully assessed and appropriately dealt with – but first we need to identify what factors do influence early sexual activity among adolescents.

Adolescent risk taking in sexual behaviours

Early sexual activity: prevalence and implications

The situation in the UK

Ongoing public concern about indiscriminate sexual risk behaviours among young people is provoked by the high rate of teenage pregnancies and their associated multiple repercussions. Apart from the potential direct consequences of unplanned and unwanted pregnancies, this behaviour increases the incidence of adolescent morbidity related to abortions, pelvic inflammatory disease with the risk of infertility later in adulthood, foetal losses and the risk of psychological trauma (Munro *et al.*, 2004). An equally important concern is the vulnerability of this group to Sexually Transmitted Diseases (STDs) and HIV. These are examined in more detail below.

An epidemiological profile of the general population of the UK has revealed that young people under sixteen years of age form a distinct high risk group where STDs and their associated complications are concerned. At the same time, the rate of pregnancy among thirteen to fifteen year old girls was reported to have stabilised at around ten per 1,000 during the period 1990 to 2000 (NATSAL, 2000). The national statistical figures for Scotland show that pregnancy rates among young adolescents, of thirteen to fifteen years of age, have been fluctuating since the mid-1990s with rates between 9.8 per 1,000 in 1996–7 and 7.5 per 1000 in 2003–4. Among the older teenage group, of sixteen to nineteen years of age, rates are declining. The highest rates were recorded in Tayside – 10.3 per 1,000, Dumfries and Galloway – 9.3 per 1000 and Fife – 9.0 per 1000. Conception rates by age show consistent increases among young adolescents of thirteen and fourteen years of age (Register General for Scotland Annual Reports, 2001).

How does the UK compare to other countries?

International figures compiled by UNICEF in 2001 showed that, among the developed countries, the US had the highest teenage pregnancy rate of 50 per 100,000 among girls of fifteen to nineteen years of age. However, the UK pregnancy rate of 31 per 100,000 represented the highest rate in Europe. The pregnancy outcomes of births, abortions and foetal losses tend to reflect the rates of conception. The crucial questions, however, are what factors influence teenage sexual activities, their attitudes and behaviours.

Pre-teen and teenage pregnancy

First sexual intercourse: opportunistic behaviour?

First sexual intercourse

A recent investigation revealed that, in the UK, the overall average age at first sexual intercourse has dropped from seventeen to sixteen years of age. In relation to the timing, age and gender variations, 30% of teenage males and 26% of teenage females reported to have engaged in sexual intercourse before the age of sixteen. Among the females, however, the incidence of this behaviour appears to have remained more stable over the past decade (NATSAL, 2000). In examining adolescents' sexual competence based on autonomy of personal sexual decision, use of contraception, willingness and regret, the findings show limited sexual competence among those who engage in intercourse at thirteen to fifteen years of age. The pattern of relationships in such sexual behaviours is that adolescents who fall into that category are more likely to engage in risky practices with multiple and concurrent sexual partners and are unlikely to use contraceptive protection during their first intercourse. The links between the factors thus created are illustrated in Figure 4.1.

Figure 4.1

Interlinked factors associated with risky adolescent sexual behaviours

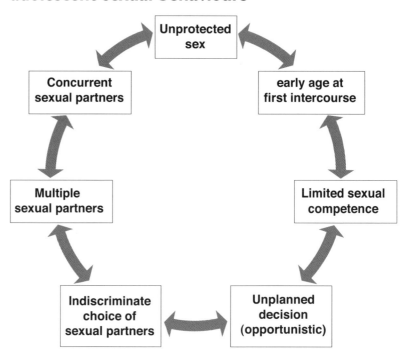

Adolescent risk taking in sexual behaviours

These behaviours are noted to be more common among adolescent males than among adolescent females. In reality, age at first sexual intercourse has progressively declined so that currently nearly one in five adolescent females and one in four adolescent males experience sexual intercourse before the legal age of sexual consent. Clearly, the potential impact on adolescents' sexual health and overall morbidity becomes a significant concern for society and, perhaps more importantly, for service providers and policy-makers in the move to reduce sexual risks (NATSAL, 2000; Sieving *et al.*, 2006).

Sexual risk behaviours

Sexual risk behaviours

Sexual risk behaviours encompass actions that increase the likelihood of harmful sexual health outcomes. The latest, more refined definition of sexual health incorporates three fundamental elements of sexual health:

i. the capacity to express sexuality, enjoy and control sexual and reproductive behaviour responsibly, in fulfilling emotional relationships, while respecting personal and social moral codes and principles

ii. the right to control fertility with freedom from unfounded fear, guilt and misconceptions that may constrain sexual response and compromise sexual relationship, and

iii. freedom from organic diseases and deficiencies that adversely affect sexual and reproductive functions (WHO, 2002).

These recognise the diversity of sexuality in society while advocating the fulfilment of positive sexual health and general wellbeing rather than focusing on sexual disorders, dysfunction and STDs. A closer examination of the WHO definition suggests that sexual health risk may be influenced by sexual behaviours, attitudes and social factors, as well as biological risks, genetic predisposition and mental health.

The extent to which adolescents take precautions to protect themselves from problems such as STDs/HIV infection and unintended or unwanted pregnancies may reflect various factors.

Pre-teen and teenage pregnancy

Influencing factors

Factors influencing risk-taking behaviours include personal, social and environmental aspects of young people's lives (Sieving *et al.*, 2006):

- factors relating to the family situation, for example:
  - living with a single parent
  - maternal history of adolescent pregnancy and childbirth
  - poor parental supervision and support
  - having older sexually active siblings or siblings with a history of adolescent conception and birth
  - family disruption
- low socio-economic status
- peer pressure
- poor educational achievement
- truancy
- dropping out of school
- media influence.

Various studies have established a link between adolescent sexual risk behaviours and certain family situations with consequences of unintended or unwanted pregnancies. Particular influencing factors are single parent families with inconsistent or poor supervision and support (Miller *et al.*, 1997) and sexually active adolescent siblings who have experienced pregnancy and childbirth (East and Felice, 1992; East, 1996).

A considerable proportion of young adolescents in the thirteen to fifteen age group may be exposed to factors that restrict their ability to make informed sexual and reproductive health choices. Cultural and ethno-racial values and beliefs may have a strong impact on the behaviours and attitudes of a particular group of adolescents before the legal age of consent and marriage. Evidence shows that, among some ethnic groups, the social context within which the adolescents are brought up may be rigidly controlled by cultural and religious values and beliefs. Within those social environments the adolescent girl may be at risk of early marriage and childbearing while others may be restricted from the freedom related to sexual development and maturity. Each of these scenarios could have both positive and negative impacts on sexuality, sexual behaviours and sexual health of the adolescents (http://www.youthinformation.com).

Adolescent risk taking in sexual behaviours

Among some ethnic groups, pressure and anxiety to know that they are fertile may cause adolescent girls to engage in the risk of early sexual intercourse to test their fertility status. The additional potential risk consequent to this behaviour is the likely termination of the pregnancy, although not in all cases.

Among other social groups, there may be pressure on teenagers to move out of the family home, based on the adolescent's perceived need for independence. This may result in sexual risk-taking with a desperate need to become pregnant. The motive in this case is to attain prioritisation for council accommodation but the implication is that such teenagers would fall into the category of welfare dependency. That preoccupation is often associated with carelessness in sexual behaviours and possible exposure to the adverse consequences of physical, sexual, emotional, psychological and mental trauma as well as infections and disease. The question arises as to what proportion of teenage pregnancies occurs unintentionally and what proportion occurs by design? In many cases, the associated factors may be related to the individual's personality, cognitive and biological maturity and sexuality. The risk behaviour may be related to:

● lack of knowledge of sexual health risks
● unrealistic health beliefs and lack of a clear perception of what constitutes risky sexual behaviours
● lack of knowledge of the associated consequences and the potential impact on their general health
● lack of self-confidence and poor interpersonal negotiation skills with the sexual partner at the time of intercourse.

These increase the vulnerability of such adolescents and they are likely to engage in their first and subsequent sexual intercourse without taking appropriate precautions. In fact, many do not give much thought to the potential outcomes or the health implications of their behaviours (Plant and Plant, 1992; Rigsby *et al.*,1998).

Consequences of adolescent sexual risk behaviours

Sexual risk behaviours

Evidence from the literature reveals a national and international concern about the potential consequences associated with risky sexual behaviours among young people.

Pre-teen and teenage pregnancy

The main consequences include:

- STDs and HIV
- Pelvic Inflammatory Disease with complications of ectopic pregnancies and infertility
- unintended and unwanted pregnancies, abortions and premature births
- psychological consequences of sexual coercion and abuse
- poor educational, social and economic opportunities for the teenage mother (Rigsby *et al.*, 1998).

These conditions usually result in increased attendance at GP surgeries and sexual health clinics for medical consultation and treatment. Additionally, the high rate of unintended pregnancies may result in consultations to seek emergency contraception or termination of the pregnancies. The nature of the request may depend on the stage of the pregnancy at the time of the consultation. Some adolescents may conceal the fact that they have conceived and therefore delay the initial medical consultation. Such delays are mainly attributable to uncertainty, confusion and fear of how the parents may react to the situation.

However, some studies have revealed that there may be a trend of repeat adolescent pregnancies following the first episode of early adolescent pregnancy. For example the Social Exclusion Unit (1999) noted that 10 % of sixteen- to nineteen-year-old adolescents who present for termination of pregnancy have a history of previous abortion. Other research findings have also revealed that following the first episode of early adolescent pregnancy some of this group are likely to present with repeat pregnancies within a relatively short period while still in their teens. Those teenagers engage in that risk behaviour irrespective of whether the previous pregnancy resulted in childbirth, termination of pregnancy, miscarriage or other foetal losses (Rigsby *et al.*, 1998).

STDs

Sexually Transmitted Diseases

STDs continue to pose significant sexual and general health problems not only for those affected but also for the whole of society. Because of the mode of acquisition and the social stigma many adolescents may feel ashamed, embarrassed or guilty about having acquired an STD and therefore shy away from seeking medical treatment. Delay in seeking testing and treatment could also be associated with lack of adequate knowledge or being asymptomatic and therefore unaware of having contracted the infection. Yet many of these infections can be successfully cured if detected early and treated.

Evidence from communicable disease surveys reveals that adolescents from thirteen to nineteen years of age are a particularly high risk group and one in four new STDs are diagnosed in teenagers. This age group, and young adults of twenty to twenty-four years of age, are the most vulnerable. The following factors contribute to the high rates among young people:

- being more sexually active

- having multiple and/or concurrent sexual partners

- indiscriminate choice of sexual partners and therefore having sex with individuals who may be at high risk of STDs

- engaging in unprotected sexual intercourse (PHLS, 2001).

It has become clearly evident that reproductive health problems account for up to 15% of diseases in the world (PHLS, 2001).

In devising sexual risk assessment tools and interventional programmes account ought to be taken of these factors to enhance the effectiveness of the measures employed in dealing with the problems. In addition to the prescribed drug and other related treatments, it is also crucial that those affected establish and maintain contact with appropriately qualified healthcare practitioners. These professionals provide evidence-based advice, support and guidance through expertly designed health education programmes to help young people to avoid being re-infected.

The danger of neglecting to seek treatment is that certain STDs can progress beyond the affected reproductive structures to involve other organs in the body causing more serious and life-threatening, long-term and debilitating conditions. Examples of related complications include:

- Pelvic Inflammatory Disease (PID)

- damage to reproductive structures

- risk of ectopic pregnancy

- infertility

- risk of cervical and other genital cancers

- foetal complications if pregnancy has occurred

- recurrent genital infections

● rarely, hepatitis and other chronic liver disease/cancer

(National Strategy for Sexual Health and HIV (DH, 2001).

Furthermore, apart from the individuals themselves, an equally important implication is that delay in seeking treatment can result in further spread of the infections to other contacts (Munro *et al.*, 2004). The following section examines the common STDs to which young people are at high risk. Rather than a detailed description of the course of each infection the main issues examined are the prevalence, transmission and health implications where the population of adolescents and young adults are concerned.

Chlamydia infection

Chlamydia infection

Chlamydia trachomatis is one of the commonest genital infections affecting females. It can result in serious complications in other parts of the body which implies that not only is the reproductive morbidity increased but that 39% of females diagnosed with Pelvic Inflammatory Disease (PID) report a previous chlamydia infection. There is also evidence that the incidence of genital hlamydia had more than doubled among adolescent females who attended Genito-Urinary Medicine (GUM) clinics between 1991 and 1999 (CDSC, 2001). The rate continues to rise among young people and is most prevalent among females of sixteen to nineteen years of age. Between 2001 and 2002 there was a 66% increase in the number of adolescent females under sixteen years of age who were diagnosed with a chlamydia infection.

Many affected males and females do not experience any symptoms and so are unlikely to attend GUM clinics for treatment, with the risk of further spread among the population of young people who engage in sexual risk behaviours. Healthcare professionals are more aware of the prevalence of this infection and improved scientific and technological advancements have resulted in better tests for diagnosing new cases. Clearly there is a need for more extensive screening programmes with health promotion and health education campaigns if most cases are to be identified and treated.

Gonorrhoea

Gonorrhoea

Gonorrhoea is an STD caused by the bacterium neisseria gonorrhoea. Similarly to chlamydia, gonorrhoea can infect the cervix, uterus, uterine tubes, rectum, urethra as well as the mouth and throat of affected females, although males can also be affected. The infection can be transmitted through risky sexual activities during vaginal, anal and oral sex. It can present without symptoms in up to 90% of females and therefore transmission and acquisition can occur without either partner being aware of it. Transmission can also occur through various modes other than direct contact, for example through infected hands, sharing of clothing and towels and can be transmitted from mother to baby, during or even after vaginal delivery. This is because the bacteria can survive for a considerable period – up to four hours outside the body (CDSC, 2001).

Although the prevalence and the rate of gonorrhoea appeared to decline in the early 1990s, this changed from the mid-1990s. The highest incidence is reported among fifteen- to nineteen-year-old adolescent females and the rate was found to have doubled in the period between 1994 and 1999 among the sixteen- to nineteen-year-old group (Munro *et al.*, 2004). With some geographical variations, the increases in rate and distribution among young people have shown a common pattern. This is also related to the sexual risk behaviours of young people.

The characteristic symptoms can be confused with other vaginal infections or urinary tract infection. An asymptomatic female may not be aware of being the source of infection until she is tracked through her infected partner. Symptomatic females may experience the following within ten days of the infection:

- painful sexual intercourse
- low abdominal or pelvic pain
- burning sensation during urination
- yellowish-green vaginal discharge
- bleeding from the vagina
- vulval tenderness
- fever and arthritic pain.

Male symptoms may manifest within five days of acquiring the infection and include:

- swollen and painful testicles
- yellowish-white discharge from the penis
- burning sensation during urination
- fever (CDSC, 2001).

In both the affected females and males, infection of the lower bowel may cause painful bowel movement, blood stained purulent discharge from the rectum as well as anal itching with soreness and bleeding.

Genital herpes simplex viral infection (HSV)

Genital herpes

Genital herpes, which is caused by the herpes simplex virus type 2 (HSV-2), is common among adolescent females and young adult females. The prevalence of genital herpes simplex among the adolescent female group has increased by 54% in recent years. In 2001, the rate among adolescent females was second highest after the rate for the young female adults of 20 to 24 years of age (CDSC, 2001).

The pattern of transmission is complex and seems to be associated with particular practices of sexual activity. The main mode of transmission is through direct skin to skin contacts through infected secretions. The herpes virus types 1 and 2 are transmitted through sexual activity. Adolescent pregnant girls with active primary genital herpes carry the risk of infecting the foetus/newborn baby. The main sites of infection therefore reflect the nature of sexual practices in which the individual has engaged. Commonly affected sites in females include the cervix and vulva and in males the glans penis and the prepuce. In both genders other sites of infection associated with the sexual practices may be the rectum, anus, perineum and the mouth may also be affected. The characteristic symptoms are that at onset of the infection the adolescent may experience tenderness, itching and a burning sensation in the affected area (CDSC, 2001).

The interventional strategies employed should take account of the fact that primary and recurrent infections can occur without manifestation of the characteristic symptoms. If these occur they are likely to be less severe and resolve within a relatively short period.

Genital warts

Genital warts

These are caused by the human papilloma virus (HPV) and described as the most common sexually transmitted disease in the world and the most commonly diagnosed STD in the UK. It is also estimated that up to 70% of sexually active women are infected and that includes those who may have been exposed to only limited sexual contacts. The descriptive names indicate the different sites commonly affected. Therefore, genital warts may be described as anogenital warts, vulval warts, labial warts, vaginal warts, cervical warts or, in the male, penile warts.

Other sites that may be affected are the rectum, anus and scrotum. Several strains of the organism have been identified in genital infections and characteristic symptoms depend on the type of HPV. Typical skin growths may appear in and around the affected structures in the genital area and the person may present no symptoms until the growth appears. Untreated and progressive growth of the warts can obstruct the openings of the vagina, anus and urethra. In other types of HPV the characteristic symptoms may be abnormal cell changes (for example, precancerous stage occurs in the cervix). In genital warts the main mode of transmission is through sexual contact (Corey and Handsfield, 2000). Numerous types of the virus have been identified but the particular types found to be associated with cervical cancer are types 6 and 11, described as low risk. Types 16 and 18, on the other hand, are reported as high risk HPV associated with dysplasia – the abnormal cell growth that results in 70% of cervical cancers (Gilson and Mindel, 2001).

The disturbing finding is the high prevalence among adolescents under sixteen years of age. Risk factors include early onset of sexual intercourse and multiple sexual partners which places the young adolescent female at particular risk.

HIV

HIV

The Human Immunodeficiency Virus (HIV) which causes Acquired Immune Deficiency Syndrome (AIDS) can gain access into the body through direct access into the bloodstream or through injuries or tissue damage. For example, skin tears, cuts, open sores, as well as through the mucosa in the mouth, vagina and rectum (CDSC, 2001). The commonest mode of transmission is through sexual contacts (Munro *et al.*, 2004). As such, HIV is a preventable infection but young people are at particular risk because of the prevalence of high sexual risk behaviours among this population group.

Various factors influence the rate and transmission of HIV mainly:
● increased incidence of risky sexual behaviour including unprotected sexual intercourse with an infected person

- multiple and concurrent sexual partners whose HIV status may be uncertain
- imported HIV infections through indiscriminate sexual activity with people in high risk countries during holidays abroad
- injecting drug users and the practice of sharing instruments – syringes and needles
- accidental deep puncture by HIV-contaminated instruments
- injured skin, open wounds or sores coming into contact with vaginal secretions, infected blood or semen
- transmission through non-sexual modes as in maternal to infant infection
- being treated accidentally with unscreened contaminated blood products (Scottish Executive Publications, 2003).

The main modes of transmission are sexual activities, blood-to-blood contact or mother to baby during pregnancy and delivery and breastfeeding. Therefore, the following body fluids are the main channels of contamination:

- blood
- vaginal secretions
- semen
- breast milk.

In terms of the prevalence of HIV infection, UK is described as a country of low risk. Nonetheless, from the global perspective the spread of this condition cannot be trivialised. HIV is still a significant threat to the health of a large proportion of the world population. The incidence among adolescents in the sixteen to nineteen age group was reported to be less than 2% of the newly diagnosed cases in 2001 (Scottish Executive Publications, 2003).

Evidence-based interventions

Evidence-based interventions

This final section examines the various policies, recommendations and strategies at national and local levels that are being employed to deal with the complex sexual health problems, the associated risk behaviours among young people and the potential consequences. The related dilemmas, legal and ethical implications are also examined. The intention is to address these from four key perspectives, as set out in Figure 4.2.

Figure 4.2   **Four key perspectives**

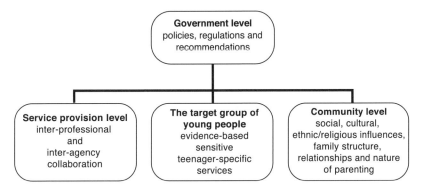

Furthermore, examples of selected practices will be reviewed and, where feasible, an exemplar presented to illustrate appropriate tools and guiding principles. The National Strategy for Sexual Health and Relationships (2002) outlined three main aims:

● to find ways to reduce the levels of unintended pregnancies and sexually transmitted infections

● to improve the way sexual health services were provided

● to promote better understanding of sexual health.

The view was that, to achieve these aims successfully from a broad perspective, it would be necessary to take account of the wider influences which affect the sexual health of the general population. Therefore, education, self-esteem, equality, social inclusion as well as the problems of alcohol and substance misuse, homelessness and domestic abuse were identified as the main concerns that needed to be prioritised.

This view evidently acknowledged the need for:

● a more positive attitude and respect for sexuality and diversity

● recognition of the influences that economic, social and cultural factors have on sexual wellbeing and the need to eliminate the associated inequalities

● providing opportunities for lifelong learning and employment to attain career aspirations and build self-esteem

● opportunities for learning about relationships and the moral implications relating to sex, sexual health, and how to access appropriate services

● provision of supportive, accessible and confidential services

(DH, 2002).

Pre-teen and teenage pregnancy

Policies and regulations

The complexity of implementing effective sexual healthcare services to meet the needs of young people is widely acknowledged. While sexual health used to be generally considered as an integral part of reproductive health, it became necessary for the WHO to review that policy based on the global pandemic of HIV infection and consistently rising rates of certain forms of STDs. Additionally, gender-related violence and sexual dysfunction were being more openly brought up as issues of significant societal concern. To ensure that sexual health issues were dealt with efficiently, the WHO's Department of Reproductive Health and Research came to the decision that sexual health ought to be considered as a separate unit or entity.

In that context the field of sexual health encompasses:

● STDs, HIV and Reproductive Tract Infections (RTIs)

● unintended pregnancy and unsafe abortion

● infertility

● sexual wellbeing (including sexual satisfaction, pleasure, and dysfunction)

● violence related to gender and sexuality

● certain aspects of mental health

● the impact of physical disability and chronic illness on sexual health

● female genital mutilation.

(WHO, 2004)

Its aim is to give recognition to sexuality among all social groups while promoting optimal sexual health and safer sex. It was envisaged that the new set up would help to:

● build the evidence base for high quality non-discriminatory, acceptable and sustainable sexual health education and service programmes;

● increase knowledge and understanding of the social and cultural factors related to harmful sexual practices in order to develop strategies to abolish these practices.

(WHO, 2004)

These objectives pose particular challenges for various sectors of service providers including the health service, social work service, education authorities, the local authorities, youth organisations, the family and community service providers. There are issues of moral and ethical sensitivity with related legal implications which create uncertainties and a reluctance by some policymakers, service providers and practitioners to address and deal with specific aspects of young people's sexual health needs at all levels with confidence. There is, therefore, a need for a comprehensive and holistic framework to guide policy and practice.

The National Sexual Health and Relationships Strategy recognises and advocates provision of appropriate sexual health services for meeting the needs of the socially excluded. That requires informed consideration of the potential impact of ethnicity, deprivation and socio-economic influences. It also advocates the importance of recognising and implementing more effective means of dealing with stigmatisation and discrimination relating to HIV and sexuality (DH, 2001). These are ongoing issues relating to young people and therefore, cannot be treated with complacency.

While not advocating teenage pregnancies, the UK government has demonstrated its support in terms of funding for teenage pregnancy strategies that take account of aspects of successful practices in Europe and the US. This has allowed for the implementation of research and training programmes not only for setting up services but also for preparing healthcare practitioners as well as teachers and youth workers to enable them to provide efficient support, sexual health promotion, education and counselling to all groups of young people and specifically targeting pregnant adolescent and young adult females. Hadley (2004) justifies the need for a teenage pregnancy strategy by indicating the statistical rates of 75% unplanned pregnancies and 46% abortions. Furthermore, she points out the serious situation in the UK where contraceptive use among this vulnerable, high risk group is notably inconsistent despite the relatively high prevalence of STDs associated with the sexual risk behaviours.

To that end, the National Sexual Health Advisory Committee's strategy for sexual health is aimed at monitoring media campaigns, advocacy interventions and literacy. In addition, it argues for media campaigns to promote equality, respect and recognition of diversity and to emphasise the potential benefits of using the barrier method of contraception with other methods to improve protection against STDs and unintended and unwanted pregnancies (Hermiston, 2004)

Sex and Relationships Education

Sex and relationships education

Sex and Relationships Education (SRE) forms a fundamental component of the broad topic of sexual and reproductive health. This discussion of adolescent sexual health would be found lacking if this crucial aspect of human sexuality was not addressed. To contextualise this concept in the discussion of sexual health this section begins with a brief examination of what SRE means and what it involves.

> It is lifelong learning about physical, moral and emotional development. It is about the understanding of the importance of marriage for family life, stable and loving relationships, respect, love and care. It is also about the teaching of sex, sexuality, and sexual health. It is not about the promotion of sexual orientation or sexual activity – this would be inappropriate teaching. (DfEE, 2000)

The general concern about adolescent sexual health is clearly obvious, through various ongoing debates and extensive in-depth discussions. Young people must be provided sound information, guidance and expert support by those who have their best interest and welfare at heart. In the DfEE definition, SRE incorporates three key components:

● attitudes and values

● personal and social skills, and

● knowledge and understanding.

Under attitudes and values, SRE involves learning and developing personal conscience and moral development, the value of family life, marriage and stable relationships, respect, love and care, as well as raising the young people's awareness about moral dilemmas whilst fostering critical thinking skills and decision-making.

In relation to personal and social skills, it involves learning how to deal with emotions confidently and sensitively within relationships, developing self-respect and empathy and learning how to make reasoned, non-judgemental choices without prejudice. It also involves learning to accept personal responsibility for one's own choices and decisions and how to deal with conflicts whilst recognising the importance of justice and fairness.

Under knowledge and understanding, SRE involves learning about the stages of human growth and maturity, gaining an understanding of sexuality, reproduction and sexual health and what contraception means and gaining an awareness of the services provided to support and advise on sexual health. It also involves acquiring an understanding of the reasons for delaying sexual activity and the possible consequences of engaging in early sexual activity (DfEE, 2000).

While some aspects of this may sound idealistic and perhaps raise concerns for parents and teachers, these areas are nonetheless crucial for supporting young people in their development. Knowledge about the different issues will enable young people to seek clarifications in order to avoid confusion and acting on mythical notions about sex and sexuality and the acquired understanding would help them to express their concerns, ask pertinent questions and seek guidance and support.

The DfEE issues guidance for schools to develop their own up-to-date policies for implementing SRE and encourages them to involve parents and make the programme descriptor, detailing the content and specifications of the programme, available to them and to education inspectors. They consider that SRE should be an integral part of the Personal, Social and Health Education framework and reflect the Social Exclusion Unit's report on teenage pregnancy (DfEE, 2000). The guidelines also recommend that it should apply equally to both genders whatever their circumstances. This is an improvement and a move away from the traditional practice that concentrates on adolescent females who are pregnant, have had an abortion or given birth.

The staged SRE programme should have learning at pre-pubertal stage, learning at the transitional stage of puberty followed by appropriate learning from then on, when more complex, sensitive issues are examined with the older adolescents. This strategy will ensure that girls understand the physiological processes of menstruation and that they are prepared and supported for the associated emotional and psychological effects.

The school SRE policy should advocate that awareness is raised among all the pupils, both the pre-teens and the teenagers, about STDs and their prevention. At an appropriate stage there should be a component of learning about safer sex. Additionally the school policy should include providing explanation about the moral and personal dilemmas associated with abortion and the potential psychological impact that can result from that experience.

Sexual abuse and trauma through rape can have devastating impact on the victim and, therefore, it is crucial that these are sensitively dealt with by relevant experts. The referral processes should also be dealt with sensitively to avoid further trauma. Apart from the mental and psychological trauma and emotional turmoil of sadness, guilt, anger and frustration, the adolescent victim may have the additional burden of being exposed to various moral, ethical and legal, possibly cultural and religious conflicts and humiliating procedures. Confidentiality is vital in such cases at every stage from the initial interviews to obtain a detailed history. Support, guidance and ongoing expert counselling should be provided by a qualified professional. A clinical psychologist is likely to be involved and the support of the parents and siblings should be encouraged. The parents may require support, education and guidance as well as counselling from relevant qualified professionals to provide a multi-disciplinary team approach to care.

Confidentiality issues should be clearly outlined in the school policy and, in addition to following their own professional codes and regulations, the health professionals who work in the schools should comply with the school policy on confidential matters. Responsibility for SRE should not lie solely with schools but be shared between schools, parents and the wider community (DfEE, 2000).

The guidelines recommend that adolescent fathers should also receive appropriate sex and relationships education. If it is delivered within the context of the Personal, Social and Health Education framework of the school curriculum this should be feasible. Another recommendation is that delivery of the programme should be staged from primary school level onwards. There should be careful monitoring of SRE programmes by the OFSTED inspectors in compliance with the statutory requirement of the School Inspections Act 1996.

The aim is to ensure that the programmes that are designed to meet the needs of adolescents and young people reflect a multi-professional and inter-agency approach. As appropriate, they should involve participation by the target group, their families, the local community, peers, the education providers, voluntary organisations, and the media (DH, 2003).

The Sexual Health Strategy for Scotland (2003) also proposes measures for achieving more effective Sexual Health Promotion as part of the SRE programme. The key elements are that there should be a national campaign to support parents to be able to talk to their children about sex. It suggests that successful practices be disseminated with guidelines for training other mothers.

Young people should be helped to develop and use appropriate social skills in their relationships and they should be supported in their pursuit of their aims and aspirations. There is also a recommendation that a suitable environment should be established to encourage young people to articulate their values, levels of respect, perceived responsibilities, and relationships with their parents, peers and teachers. They should feel comfortable in that setting to openly discuss their perceptions of the ways in which the media portrays sex and relationships. This may help to gain better insight of their views in order to answer their questions, clarify any misconceptions, address their particular concerns and provide appropriate guidance and support (Scottish Executive Publications, 2003a,b,c).

In delivering SRE, the health strategy advocates use of IT and visual aids to convey accurate and realistic information about key issues and to create a conducive and non-threatening atmosphere that encourages young people to express their thoughts. Professionals who coordinate these sessions should be well informed and experienced in working with young people in order to address the different issues at a level that makes sense to the age range and varied backgrounds of the individuals present.

Research and practice

Research and evidence-based practice

To ensure that appropriate and effective procedures are implemented to achieve successful sexual health outcomes for specific target groups healthcare practitioners, teachers, and youth workers need to identify potential research priorities (DH, 2001). Studies should be conducted to explore the factors that influence sexual risk behaviours and/or the impact of drugs and alcohol on adolescent sexual behaviours and risk-taking. Other important issues that still need further research and dissemination are the influencing and inhibiting factors associated with the health seeking behaviours of adolescents and young adults and the impact of ethnicity, deprivation and socio-economic factors on sexual health.

Evidence from a combination of qualitative and quantitative data is likely to provide a rich resource of information that could be used as the basis for developing appropriate health education programmes that address the expressed concerns and needs of young people. If appropriate and effective counselling is to be provided to enable young people to make informed choices and decisions then both the healthcare practitioners and counsellors should draw on evidence from sound research to guide the services that they provide.

Key issues to consider in a sexual health questionnaire for adolescents are outlined in Figure 4.3. The information gathered from a questionnaire along these lines would help healthcare professionals tailor their advice and guidance to the actual needs of their target group.

Health promotion and education of both young people and the wider general public are crucial to raise awareness and eliminate the social stigma associated with STDs and HIV/AIDS. This requires extensive review of the research relating to sexual health problems. Provision of sexual health services for young people invariably involves certain ethical and legal issues. Therefore careful consideration of the law and regulations – such as the Data Protection Act (1998, 2000), the Human Rights Act (1998) and the Freedom of Information Act 2000 (enforced 2005) – is also important.

Sexual health clinics

Teenager-specific sexual health clinics

Teenager-specific clinics aim to promote sensitive sexual healthcare and support to adolescents within a non-threatening environment (Jacobson and Wilkinson, 1994). The WHO advocates provision of user-friendly services, which should be accessible, user-friendly and confidential. This has been done with some success in some centres in London but it does call for careful planning and organisation of resources.

Nonetheless, the benefits of support services for the youth and effective sexual health education for groups of similar age range presenting with similar problems outweigh the costs. Effective sexual health screening with counselling, education and support services are vital within teenage specific sexual clinic settings.

Figure 4.3

Key elements of a sexual risk assessment questionnaire for adolescents

Part A
Statements to encourage reflection on, and to explore, personal sexual behaviour
- Choice of sexual partners
- Nature of preferred sexual activities
- Personal values and principles about sex

Part B
Statements designed for assessing knowledge and perceptions about sexual health
- Perception of what is sexually safe
- Perception of what is sexually risky
- Perception of what risks are most important
- Perception of what factors contribute to sexual risks
- Perception of situations in which sexual risk-taking may occur

Part C
Statements designed for assessing the social context in which the adolescent lives and functions and his/her perception of its potential influences
- Social and cultural identity
- Profile and interactions with own peer groups/circle of friends
- Perception of the group's values, principles, attitudes and way of life
- The group's views about safe sex
- Perception of what makes group members more likely to engage in sexual risks – the nature of the group's influences
- Personal views about what guiding principles and actions might help individuals or the group to achieve more effective reduction of sexual risk behaviours within the group and the community in which they live

Part D
Reflection on recent/current history of sexual activities
- Contacts and possible exposure to high risk sexual activity with a partner with dubious STD/HIV status
- Perception of current needs and intended actions

Pre-teen and teenage pregnancy

Family and community

Role of the family and community

The impact of family structure, the parenting style to which the adolescent is exposed and the nature of interaction or communication between the mother and child have a strong influence on sexual behaviour. Additionally, the social norms, cultural and religious influences, peer and media influences to which they are exposed in the community environment may have equally strong influences. Therefore, these factors need to be considered in the services implemented to support the young people. The WHO urges the following strategies within the community setting:

- comprehensive sexuality education for young people
- sexuality and sexual health training for health workers, teachers, social workers, youth workers and other key professionals
- community-based initiatives to meet the needs of out-of-school young people and others who may be especially vulnerable. (WHO, 2004)

If these are to be successfully achieved every effort should be made to implement an integrated approach to sexual healthcare provision within the primary care setting. Thus GPs, practice nurses, school nurses, health visitors, and social workers should work together to draw up strategies for implementing local sexual healthcare programmes for young people.

These programmes should take account of the range of problems and needs presented by the youth groups and should address issues relating to ethnicity, gender, cultural and religious factors and social circumstances. Such initiatives invariably, have funding implications but there are examples of strategies implemented in different parts of England and Wales, Scotland and Northern Ireland which could serve as models. In Cambridgeshire/Peterborough an integrated scheme has been developed with the aim of: 'Improving the Sexual Health of Young People in Care'. At its recent conference the team's aim was to raise awareness about sexual health and teenage pregnancy issues affecting young people looked after by the Cambridgeshire County Council Social Services Directorate and Peterborough City Council Children's Services (Education and Children) Department. Sources of funding included the Teenage Pregnancy Local Implementation Fund which is part of the Cambridgeshire/Peterborough Teenage Pregnancy strategy and the scheme was a collaboration between the Sex Education Forum, National Children's Bureau, Cambridgeshire Social Services Directorate, Peterborough City Council Education and Children, and Cambridgeshire Health Authority (http://www.cambridgeshire.gov.uk).

The need for a collaborative approach

Collaborative approach

The UK Teenage Pregnancy Strategy aims to not only reduce the rate of teenage pregnancy but also to promote the social inclusion of teenage mothers and their families. It advocates collaboration between relevant governmental, health and education departments to work towards achieving effective service provision for young people. Similarly, the Sexual Health Strategy for Scotland (2003) recommends collaborative working, with partnerships between professionals and interested agencies.

The local implementation recommended by the Scottish Executive requires that a coordinated Local Health Improvement Plan should:

- determine the pattern of teenage pregnancy by focusing on high risk areas, groups and schools
- conduct an audit of service provision
- involve local people and agencies in developing and implementing action plans to achieve the national goals
- link to other relevant local plans and initiatives such as the Healthy Living Centres and Sure Start.

(Sexual Health Strategy for Scotland, 2003)

These strategies are primarily, but not exclusively, designed to target high risk groups. In addition, the principles embedded in the strategies form the basis for better sex education, including guiding and supporting parents to discuss sex and relationships with their teenage children. Crucially, they offer guidance for improving contraceptive advice and services for young people, and, therefore, call for involving the young people in the design of the relevant services.

Other important elements are to ensure provision of better support for teenage mothers, including measures to enable them to resume their educations – particularly critical for their future career opportunities, when education becomes disrupted by pregnancy and childbirth.

Consideration is also given to the provision of effective and safe childcare facilities to help and support teenage mothers. The needs of teenage fathers are also addressed and, where possible, supported housing may be provided to ensure additional security for the adolescent mothers and their babies.

The Scottish strategy proposes additional specific requirements: the health service should promote joint working with improved communication to ensure consistent advice and direction from all relevant staff. It should also have clear aims and objectives based on its shared vision and work to plug gaps in provision and participate in shared initiatives such as promoting safe sex. Health promotion and education should be carried out with the help of health professionals. Statutory and non-statutory agencies should collaborate with other services, delivering their specific functions but also participating in shared initiatives. Service users should be persuaded to provide detailed feedback that can be used to guide improvement of the services.

Agencies such as Young Mums will also provide complementary programmes including education and guidance on aspects of health such as sexual health, child care support and guidance about welfare benefits (Young Mums, 2006). Other programmes provided by external agencies include topics such as babycare, money management, healthy living, IT skills and health and safety (Youth Information, 2006).

Such initiatives and programmes are clearly highly beneficial for young teenage mothers and fathers and for their parents and guardians but coverage is patchy. Standardisation of certain key services for teenagers across the UK is urgently needed.

Conclusion

Young people's knowledge, insight and attitudes to sexual health are significant concerns in society. Sexual behaviours among young people involve a combination of factors. These include biological factors reflecting the family context, the individual's sexuality and physical, emotional and behavioural factors including sexual orientation and cultural and religious influences. Sexuality also encompasses the social environment of the community in which the adolescent grows up and the social context of the school, including the influence of peers and close friends.

Gender convergence in sexual experience shows that the average age at first sexual intercourse is currently the same for adolescent males and females. Nevertheless, while sexual competence appears to increase among the over sixteens, the trend among under fifteens is a decline in sexual competence the younger they are.

The increasing risk of Sexually Transmitted Diseases (STDs), with a steady rise in the rates of gonorrhoea and chlamydia among sixteen- to nineteen-year-old youths, places this group high in the national and international sexual health agendas. STDs pose a particular threat to the sexual health of adolescents because of their high risk sexual behaviours and the high rates of incidence associated with many of the infections. Other related health problems may arise as complications rather than as a direct result of infections acquired through specific sexual risk behaviours.

SRE, which is an integral part of the Personal Social and Health Education framework of the school curriculum, gives due recognition to the needs of young people. It incorporates learning about sex, sexuality and sexual health, taking account of the stages of physical and cognitive growth and comprehension. The DfEE recommends that schools should develop their own policies. Whilst parents are regarded as having major authority in teaching and supporting their children about sex and relationships, training and support should be provided for those teachers and parents who express limited knowledge and confidence in doing so.

To encourage sexual health, respect and responsibility in sexual behaviour, service provision should be relevant, accessible and effective in meeting the needs of teenagers. Schools should not hold sole responsibility for SRE but involve parents and members of the wider community. Equally importantly, the perspectives of teenagers should be listened to and due consideration given to their views.

In conclusion, SRE with sexual healthcare provision should be addressed at the level of the individual, family, community and the healthcare system. This requires integrated team interventions by trained healthcare and other relevant professionals and should be based on an effective referral system in line with current legislation. In addition, we need a regulatory environment in which the sexual rights of all the service users are upheld.

References

Aggleton, P., Oliver, C. and Rivers, K. (1998) *Implications of Research into Young People, Sex, Sexuality and Relationships.* London: HEA.

Brook, C.G.D. (1981) Endocrinological control of growth at puberty. *British Medical Bulletin* **32**(3): 281–285.

Cambridgeshire County Council (2007) *The Youth Service Plan.* Available at http://www.cambridgeshire.gov.uk (accessed January 2007)

Cheesbrough, S., Ingham, R. and Massey, D. (1999) *An International Review of Evidence: USA, Canada, Australia, and New Zealand.* London: HEA

Communicable Disease Surveillance Centre (2001) *HIV, Aids and STIs in the UK: an Epidemiological Review* London: Public Health Laboratory Services.

Corey, L. and Handsfield, H.H. (2000). Genital herpes and public health: Addressing a global problem. *Journal of American Medical Association* **283**: 791–794.

Department for Education and Employment (2000) *Sex and Relationships Education Guidance.* Available at http://www.standards.dfee.gov.uk.

Department of Health (2001) *Better Prevention, Better Services, Better Sexual Health: The National Strategy for Sexual Health and HIV* London: DH.

Department of Health (2003) *Effective Sexual Health Promotion: A toolkit for Primary Care Trusts and others working in the field of promoting good sexual health and HIV prevention* London: DH.

East, P.L. (1996) Do adolescent pregnancy and childbearing affect younger siblings? *Family Planning Perspectives* **28**(4): 148–153.

East, P.L. and Felice, M.E. (1992) Pregnancy risk among the younger sisters of pregnant and childbearing adolescents. *Journal of Developmental and Behavioral Pediatrics* **13**(2): 128–136.

Gilson, J.C. and Mindel, A. (2001) Sexually Transmitted Infections. *British Medical Journal* **322**: 1160–1164.

Gruer, G. (2006) *Sexual Health: Teenage pregnancy* York: The Association of Public Health Observatories, Scottish Public Health Observatory

Hadley, A. (2004) *Sexual Health and Young People: Delivering teenage pregnancy strategies locally.* Available at http://www.westminster-briefing.com.

Health Education Authority (1999) *New Resources on Sexual Health: Reducing the rate of teenage conception* London: HEA.

Hermiston, N. (2004) *Enhancing Sexual Wellbeing in Scotland: A sexual health and relationships strategy* Edinburgh: Scottish Civic Forum.

Huebner, A. (2000) *Adolescent Growth and Development.* Petersburg: Virginia State University.

Hughes, K. (1999) *Young People's Experiences of Relationships, Sex and Early Parenthood: Qualitative research* London: HEA.

Adolescent risk taking in sexual behaviours

Jacobson, L.D. and Wilkinson, C.E. (1994) Review of teenage health: Time for a new direction. *British Journal of General Practice* **44**: 420–424.

Kane, R. and Wellings, K. (1999) *An International Review of Evidence: Data from Europe.* London: HEA.

Meyrick, J. and Swann, C. (1999) *An Overview of the Effectiveness of Interventions and Programmes Aimed at Reducing Unintended Conceptions in Young People.* London: HEA.

Miller, B.C., Norton, M. C., Curtis, T., Hill, E. J., Schvaneveldt, P. and Young, M. H. (1997) The timing of sexual intercourse among adolescents: Family, peers and other antecedents. *Youth and Society* **29**: 54–83.

Munro, H., Davis, M. and Hughes, G. (2004) Adolescent sexual health. *The Health of Children and Young People* London: ONS.

National Survey of Attitudes and Lifestyle (2000) *Teenage Pregnancy: An overview of the research evidence.* Available at http://www.wiredforhealth.gov.uk (last accessed January 2007).

Plant, M.A. and Plant, M.L. (1992) *Risktakers: Alcohol, drugs, sex and youth* London: Routledge.

Register General for Scotland (2001) Annual Reports 2001. http://www.gro-scotland.gov.uk (accessed January 2007).

Rigsby, D.C., Macones, G.A. and Driscoll, D.A. (1998) Risk factors for rapid repeat pregnancy among adolescent mothers: A review of the literature. *Journal of Pediatric and Adolescent Gynaecology* **11**:115–126.

Scottish Executive Publications (2003a) *Enhancing Sexual Wellbeing in Scotland: A Sexual Health Relationship Strategy – The wider factors influencing sexual health and wellbeing.* Available at http://www.scotland.gov.uk/Publications/2003.

Scottish Executive Publications (2003b) *A Sexual Health Relationship Strategy – Sexual health and relationships education for young people.* Available at http://www.scotland.gov.uk/Publications/2003.

Scottish Executive Publications (2003c) *Enhancing Sexual Wellbeing in Scotland: A Sexual Health Relationship Strategy – Sexual Health in Scotland: Attitudes, lifestyles and the changing epidemiology of pregnancy, abortion and sexually transmitted infections.* Available at http://www.scotland.gov.uk/Publications/2003.

Sieving, R.E., Eisenberg, M.E., Pettingell, S. and Skay, C. (2006) Friends' influence on adolescents' first sexual intercourse. *Perspectives on Sexual and Reproductive Health* **38**(1): 13–19.

Social Exclusion Unit (1999) *Teenage Pregnancy.* London: DH.

Steinberg, L. and Morris, A. S. (2001) Adolescent development. *Annual Review Of Psychology* **52**: 83–110.

Sutherland, C. (2005) Young people and sex. In Andrews, G. *Women's Sexual Health.* 3rd edn. Edinburgh: Elsevier.

The National Youth Agency (2006) *Youth Information: Teenage pregnancy.* Available at http://www.youthinformation.com.

Pre-teen and teenage pregnancy

UNICEF (2001) 'A league table of teenage births in rich nations' Innocenti Report Card 3. UNICEF Innocenti Centre: Florence.

Young Mums (2006) Available at http://www.youngmums.org.uk (accessed January 2007).

World Health Organisation (2002) *Defining Sexual Health* Geneva: WHO

World Health Organisation (2004) *Reproductive Health Strategy to Accelerate Progress Towards the Attainment of International Development Goals and Targets* Geneva: WHO.

Chapter 5
Pharmacological contraceptive prescribing for young people
Theo Kwansa

Public opinion remains divided about the provision of contraception to adolescents under sixteen years of age. Various arguments have been used to justify this policy and the persistent public concern about the high rate of teenage pregnancy seems to be the paramount justification.

There is evidence from various studies in the US that, for a considerable number of adolescent girls, the first experience of sexual intercourse is through coercion or rape. It is not surprising, then, that most girls describe their first sexual intercourse in negative terms, in terms of lack of enjoyment, regret and guilt. In some girls the issue is multifactorial. They tend to have other problems such as poor achievement at school, low self-esteem, loneliness and depression. Some of these stem from domestic problems such as dysfunctional families and emotional neglect, which contribute to making them vulnerable to being sexually abused through coercion and rape.

While there is no doubt that this does occur, changing values and attitudes in society have also had a significant impact on young people's attitudes. Cultural, religious and family values, beliefs and principles also influence young people's perceptions about their sexuality, sex and sexual health behaviours. The average age at which young people begin to demonstrate awareness of their sexuality and become sexually active seems to have dropped considerably. The implications are evident in the increasing incidence of sexual health morbidity associated with not only the unpredictable outcomes of teenage pregnancies but also Sexually Transmitted Diseases (STDs) and HIV/AIDS.

Early sex has been associated with multiple partners, placing the adolescent girl at high risk of unplanned and unwanted pregnancy, single parenthood in her early teens and Sexually Transmitted Diseases (STDs) with potential complications of Pelvic Inflammatory Disease (PID). A consequence of the unplanned pregnancy may be disruption of her education either temporarily or permanently causing her to abandon her career aspirations. Therefore, increasingly parents and society in general see contraception for the under sixteens as a necessary compromise.

The current policy of prescribing contraception to under sixteens, also stipulates young people's rights to confidentiality. It remains fraught with legal and ethical conflicts despite the detailed guidelines released by the Department of Health for doctors and other relevant health professionals.

This chapter begins with an overview of the physiology of the menstrual cycle which is then linked to a review of the different types of hormonal contraceptive methods, their modes of action and pharmacologic features, advantages, disadvantages and contraindications to highlight any evidence relating to the suitability and potential long-term risks associated with particular contraceptives for young adolescent girls. The chapter then goes on to examine the ethical and legal issues surrounding the prescribing of hormonal contraceptives for under sixteens and review government guidelines and policies.

The menstrual cycle

Hormonal influences

Hormonal influences

The key features of hormonal contraceptives are that their actions depend on the release of two synthetic steroidal hormones – oestrogens and progestogen into the body. These are similar to the ovarian oestrogens and progestogen that are naturally produced in the female's body during the menstrual cycle from puberty onwards. The ovarian production of these hormones is under the influence of Follicle Stimulating Hormone (FSH) and Luteinising Hormone (LH) from the anterior pituitary gland. The pituitary activity is also controlled by the Gonadotrophin-releasing Hormone (GnRH) produced by the hypothalamus.

Figure 5.1 shows the sources and pathways of the hypothalamic, pituitary and ovarian hormones, demonstrating how the hormones interact and how variations in levels trigger feedback mechanisms occurring in the different phases of the menstrual cycle. We will go into this in more detail as we discuss the way the various hormonal contraceptives operate.

It is always useful in clinical practice if the practitioner can draw on their knowledge base, in this case the physiology of the menstrual cycle, to explain the normal function and how the relevant treatment intervention would achieve the expected goal. A clear understanding is vital to stimulate or improve an individual's motivation to comply with the prescribed treatment. The practitioner has an obligation to ensure that the adolescent girl understands what menstruation involves and how the chosen contraceptive method would work to achieve effective protection from unwanted pregnancy and provide sex and relationships education.

The menstrual cycle encompasses two sequential events – the ovarian and endometrial cycles. These are essentially interdependent as explained below.

The ovarian cycle

The ovarian cycle

From the age of puberty (average age thirteen) Gonadotrophin-Releasing Hormone GnRH from the hypothalamus stimulates the anterior pituitary gland to produce Follicle Stimulating Hormone (FSH). This in turn causes growth and maturation of a graafian follicle in the ovary. The follicular cells produce oestrogens. As the follicle matures the serum level of oestrogens also rises. The rising level of oestrogens triggers a feedback mechanism which stimulates the anterior pituitary gland to release Luteinising Hormone (LH) while FSH production diminishes. As the serum level of the LH rises to a peak, ovulation occurs with release of the ovum from the mature follicle. Thus the ovarian cycle involves a sequence of events described as:

● the follicular phase,

● ovulation, and

● the Luteal phase (Kelly, 2003).

Figures 5.1 and 5.2 below illustrate the interactions of the hormone pathways between the ovary and pituitary gland. The timing of ovulation in relation to the surge of serum LH level may range from 10 to 30 hours and some adolescents may experience pain and discomfort – known as mittelschmerz (Kelly, 2003).

Pre-teen and teenage pregnancy

Figure 5.1   **Hormonal feedback mechanism of the ovarian cycle**

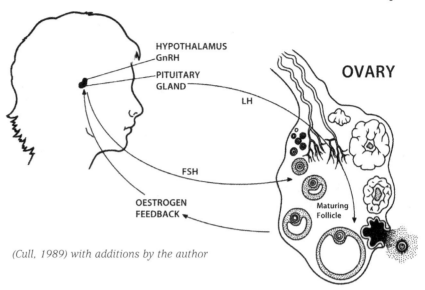

(Cull, 1989) with additions by the author

Endometrial cycle

The endometrial cycle

The oestrogens produced by the graafian follicle act on the lining of the endometrium causing regeneration and thickening – proliferation of its stroma cells and glands. Following ovulation the ruptured and collapsed follicle develops into a corpus luteum which produces large amounts of progestogen with lesser quantities of oestrogens. These two hormones, and in particular the progestogen, bring about the secretory activity of the endometrial lining causing further thickening and secretion of nutritive fluid in the glands. The endometrial blood supply also increases. As a result the endometrium may grow to a thickness of 5 to 6 mm. About ten days after ovulation, if fertilisation does not occur, the corpus luteum begins to degenerate and the levels of progestogen and oestrogen decrease progressively. The previously thickened endometrium disintegrates as a result of vasospasm and ischemia and is shed down to the basal layer during the phase of menstruation.

Like the ovarian cycle, the endometrial cycle involves three phases:
- the proliferative phase
- the secretory phase, and
- the menstrual phase (Kelly, 2003).

The duration of the menstrual cycle ranges from 25 to 35 days with an average of 28 days. The proliferative phase normally lasts ten to

14 days but may vary in adolescents who have irregular menstrual cycles. The duration of the secretory phase lasts ten days on average. Menstruation begins on day one of the menstrual cycle and may last for four to five days. These events are illustrated in Figure 5.2 below, which shows the phasic changes and the variations in hormone levels.

Figure 5.2

Pituitary and ovarian hormone fluctuations of the endometrial cycle

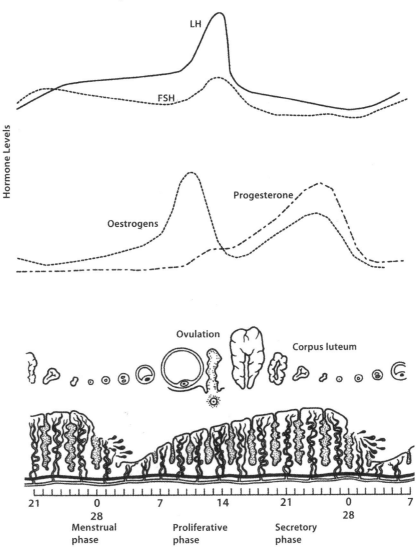

(Cull, 1989) with minor modifications by the author

Pre-teen and teenage pregnancy

Hormonal contraceptives

Several types of hormonal contraceptives are available, with different modes of adminstration:

- oral:
  - combined oral contraceptive (COC) pill
  - progestogen-only pill (POP)
- injectable
- transdermal (Patches)
- implants
- intrauterine devices
- vaginal rings

(Everett, 2005; Drugs Direct, 2000)

The main mechanisms of action of the hormonal contraceptives are similar in all the different types, although there may be variations in the extent of certain actions that occur in different types. The main actions include suppression of the hypothalamic and pituitary secretion of GnRH, FSH, and LH. The oestrogen component inhibits pituitary secretion of FSH and thus suppresses follicle growth, whilst the progestogen inhibits the LH surge that brings about ovulation. As a result the process of ovulation is inhibited and that prevents the possibility of fertilisation taking place.

Additionally, changes occur in the cervical mucus in the form of increased viscosity and low stretchiness (spinnbarkeit) and that prevents sperm transport and penetration into the uterus. This characteristic change in the cervical mucus has been reported in all the combined oral contraceptives irrespective of the dosage. Guillebaud (2000) asserts that the effectiveness of the combined hormonal preparations in achieving contraception is enhanced even if breakthrough bleeding occurs.

The third main mechanism is alteration of the endometrium. The uterine lining develops atrophic changes and becomes thin and unsuitable for implantation of a blastocyst (Everett, 2005; Wills, 2006). Guillebaud observes that with prolonged use of combined hormonal contraceptives in addition to the atrophic changes the vasculature of the endometrium also becomes reduced.

Another potential effect of the combined hormonal contraceptives occurs within the uterine tubes. The mechanism there is that alteration in the peristalsis and alteration of the tubal secretion may cause impairment of sperm migration and ovum transport.

Effectiveness and efficacy

Effectiveness and efficacy of hormonal contraceptives

Effectiveness and safety are the primary concerns among the general population when seeking guidance and advice about specific contraceptive methods. When explaining the performance of a contraceptive method to clients, it may be easier to talke about typical-use pregnancy rates rather than perfect-use rates. The typical-use rate may be a more realistic predictor of pregnancy risk for the average user.

For couples who feel strongly that pregnancy and a child would be undesirable, inconvenient or detrimental to their careers and lifestyles, the long-term and highly effective methods are likely to be their contraceptive preference (Steiner *et al.*, 1999). The practitioner is faced with the challenge of providing accurate information that takes account of the related pregnancy rates. Reference to the typical-use rates might help to make a more realistic comparison of short-term and long-term rates to help them to appreciate the effectiveness of the chosen method and the extent of their own risk of unintended pregnancy.

Similarly, adolescent girls who are sexually active but have specific future career aspirations and a strong desire to continue with their education may seek the highly effective and relatively long-term contraceptive methods. However, the latter scenario poses a particular challenge for both the client group of sexually active adolescents and the healthcare practitioners. Not only must they provide appropriate evidence-based information, support and guidance but also appropriately timed and conscientious follow up.

The Pearl Index is a statistical technique used for calculating the number of unintended pregnancies in 100 fertile women in one year (Steiner *et al.*, 1999). The technique is applied in assessing the effectiveness of the different contraceptive methods and therefore serves as a means of making comparisons. The index is used to describe two rates of measures in terms of:

efficacy – method effectiveness

This is the degree of compliance adopted by the individual in a typical use of a specific method to achieve the expected result.

effectiveness – user effectiveness

This relates to the degree of inbuilt protection that a particular contraceptive method can provide, in perfect (accurate and consistent) use, to achieve the expected result

(Steiner *et al.,* 1999).

A low Pearl Index corresponds to minimal risk of unintended pregnancy happening while the woman is using the method. However, despite its extensive use, some question its accuracy. Among the criticisms is that the calculation and the particular rates can vary between different populations in different countries. Influencing factors include demographic variables, social and economic background, culture, cognitive ability and the way the contraceptive is supplied, explained and supported.

Another limitation that has been highlighted is that certain key information is overlooked. It does not include information about the discontentment with the method or figures of the women who were trying to achieve pregnancy and women who fail to attend for follow up. Nor does it account for the fact that those women who are most fertile are likely to get pregnant while those who are least fertile would be least likely to become pregnant.

So, while a particular method may have 100% efficacy in preventing pregnancy, actual effectiveness may be much lower because of poor compliance in typical use by clients. Therefore, to achieve the desired effectiveness and perfect efficacy, the user must be highly motivated to use the method correctly and conscientiously. Crucially, the user must pay careful attention to every detail in the instructions and guidelines.

Interference with absorption and utilisation of oral contraceptive pills

- Inconsistent use of the contraceptive method
- Incorrect use of the contraceptive method
- Lack of supply or problems with continued availability
- Ability of the client to go for further supply
- Limited access to obtain repeat prescriptions
- The motivation of the client
- Ability to take appropriate action in situations such as missed pills or problems with the menstruation

- Lack of clarity of practitioners' explanations, instruction and guidance (Steiner *et al.*, 1999)
- Inadequate absorption through such things as diarrhoea and vomiting
- Drug interaction can also disrupt absorption and utilisation of oral contraceptives.

Combined oral contraceptive pills (COC)

Combined pills

The combined oral contraceptive pills consist of synthetic versions of the ovarian steroids – oestrogens and progestogen – described in the ovarian and endometrial cycles above. The synthetic component of oestrogens is referred to as ethinylestradiol and the synthetic of progestogen is progestogens which are produced in different forms. Therefore, the differences in the available brands may be determined by the composition of oestrogens and progestogens in terms of the dosage of each component, and the type or preparation of progestogen used in the particular brand or product of combined oral contraceptive (Drug Digest, 2000; Guillebaud, 2000). Since lower doses of oestrogens have been found to be associated with fewer side effects, most combined oral contraceptives in current use contain carefully calculated small quantities of these steroids.

Combined oral contraceptives may be described as monophasic, biphasic or triphasic. The two latter preparations were developed with the aim of reducing the dosage of steroids in the pills. The main purpose of the phasic preparations is to minimise the incidence of hormone-related side effects and so achieve better user compliance. The phasic preparations are claimed to be more reliable at achieving withdrawal bleed although many women may find it difficult to grasp the procedure relating to missed pills.

The *monophasic* combined hormonal contraceptive is the most widely used type. This preparation, which contains equal dosage of oestrogens and progestogen in all the pills taken in the cycle, is found to be associated with fewer complications and is relatively simple for users. Therefore, its better compliance rate helps to achieve higher reliability (Guillebaud, 2000; Drug Digest, 2000).

The *biphasic* type is designed to provide a higher dosage of oestrogens in the first seven days. The amount of progestogen, however, increases in the second half of the cycle. The purpose is to improve cycle control. Additionally, the biphasic preparations have been found to benefit women who present with problems of breakthrough bleeding and acne. This type of oral contraceptive has to be taken conscientiously to achieve the desired effectiveness. In terms of dosage, although the amount of oestrogens remains constant throughout the cycle package the amount of progestogen varies at different stages of the cycle.

The principle of the *triphasic* preparation is to act in a similar way to the oestrogens and progestogen in the normal menstrual cycle. Whilst the amount of oestrogen may remain constant or vary, the progestogen dosage increases in three stages. Although the endometrial changes produced by this type of COC are claimed to be closer to the changes in a normal cycle, experts have found no substantive evidence that this achieves better cycle control (Guillebaud, 2004).

Effectiveness and efficacy

Guillebaud observes that the reliability of the combined oral contraceptive pill is nearly 100% (99.9%) if the client takes it consistently and follows the instructions correctly. The failure rate is reported as 0.2 to 3.0 per 100 woman years. Experts also note that client errors in taking the contraceptive pill may be more common than they actually report. Thus typical failure rates may range between 3 and 8%. However, careful interviewing can reveal the reason for unforeseen contraceptive failure and pregnancy. It has also been reported that COCs have an increased failure for women over 70 kg in weight but this claim remains controversial because of lack of substantive research evidence.

Advantages and disadvantages

The advantages, including non-contraceptive benefits, and disadvantages of COCs are outlined in Table 5.1. They will vary between different pills and they may also reflect individuals' tolerance and personal preferences.

Table 5.1

Advantages and disadvantages of COCs

Advantages

Key advantages and non-contraceptive benefits:

- reliable/reversible/convenient/ independent of sexual intercourse
- more regular periods with less bleeding
- reduced incidence of menorrhagia with reduced incidence of iron deficiency anaemia associated with the heavy menstrual losses
- reduced menstruation-related problems such as Pre-Menstrual Syndrome
- reduced incidence of ovulation pain and dysmenorrhoea
- reduced incidence of Pelvic Inflammatory Disease

Other possible advantages:

- reduced incidence of benign breast disease
- reduced incidence of functional ovarian cysts/improved control of polycystic ovary syndrome
- improvement in acne and other seborrhoeic problems

Some protective benefits

- notable protection against cancers of the ovaries and the endometrium
- reported protection against thyroid disease, rheumatoid arthritis and trichomonal vaginitis

Disadvantages

Risk of being predisposed to side effects such as thromboembolic disease with increased risk of

- pulmonary embolism
- deep vein thrombosis
- cerebral thrombosis
- leg injury and tissue damage, e.g. following surgery on the leg, with immobility that may also be a contributory factor to the risk of DVT

NB The previously higher incidences of thromboembolic disease, DVT, pulmonary embolism and stroke have been reduced in current users of COC. Most preparations now contain minimum doses of Ethinyloestradiol (20–35 µg)

Notable association between idiopathic venous thromboembolism and current smoking, excessive weight (BMI > 35) and asthma:

- increased risk of ischaemic stroke
- increased risk of coronary thrombosis in older women who smoke heavily (> one pack per day)

therefore, increased age does become a risk factor

- contested possible risk of myocardial infarction.

Practical considerations

Oral contraceptives are found by many women to be relatively easy to use and this popularity is partly attributable to the fact that the timing is independent of sexual intercourse. This may be one of the reasons why young women, including adolescents, might choose this method as a preferred option. Various studies have shown that COC can achieve maximum protection from pregnancy (Guillebaud, 2004) but the importance of compliance should be emphasised by practitioners when providing advice and instructions to clients.

In the UK, COCs are reported as being the most popular choice of contraception among young women between 19 and 30 years of age. Its reversibility and reliability and other potential benefits, lead many couples to choose this method of contraception in planning their families. They do, however, need to understand the possible variations in reversibility if they are keen to start a family later. The healthcare practitioner must explain the issue clearly to avoid disappointment. Older teenage girls from the cultural backgrounds where marriage and family is a major expectation may experience anxiety and concern about the uncertainty of their fertility status (Kumar, 1998). Although the practitioner may not be the first resort, such girls may occasionally seek counselling and support or request a means of finding out. The practitioner has an equal duty to listen sympathetically in order to be able to address this client problem sensitively.

Client concerns about potential adverse effects and possible long-term complications relating to COC should not be dismissed as they may be based on rational fears. A client may be concerned about the implications of an existing medical condition, treatment medication, family history, or recent media claims of research findings about specific complications. Society expects appropriately qualified healthcare practitioners to be able to provide explanations based on sound research evidence to ensure careful decision-making and to guide clients in making informed choices.

It is the duty of the practitioner to discuss the benefits of the COC if that is the contraceptive of choice and whether it is suitable for the particular client. It is also the practitioner's duty to provide reassurance but the final decision should be made by the person or the couple, even where teenagers are concerned. It is important to answer questions correctly, provide clarifications and provide reassurance to dispel anxieties. It is also the duty of the practitioner to guide clients about avoidance of sexual health risks, and the importance of practicing safe sex and safer sexual health lifestyle and behaviours. People need to be convinced that the guidance they receive would help to reduce their risks of acquiring infections.

Guillebaud (2004) recommends that healthcare practitioners should keep up-to-date through research, CPD courses, study days, workshops or in-service training programmes. These requirements of ongoing post registration education and training ventures may be embedded in sections of the codes of professional practice and are crucial (NMC, 2004; DH, 2004). These are designed to encourage and guide practitioners in the ongoing development of their professional knowledge and skills. Arguably, it is only through a habit of exploring the relevant literature that greater insight and understanding can be gained about findings from current research on specific topics such as success with new practices, treatment protocols and new procedures. It is also by engaging in such professional activities that practitioners' awareness may be raised about national guidelines and areas of research priorities for ongoing improvement of practice.

Related side effects

- Nausea
- Vomiting
- Headaches
- Possible raised blood pressure
- Breast tenderness
- Fluid retention with weight gain
- Possible skin changes – chloasma
- Reduced menstrual loss

(British National Formulary, 2005)

Phasic presentations

Figure 5.3 below is an example of monophasic preparation of combined oral contraceptive. This is presented in a schedule of 21 days and followed by seven days of no pill-taking.

Figure 5.3

Presentation of the Monophasic COC – Microgynon

> **Microgynon 30**
>
> **21 tablets in the schedule, each tablet containing:**
>
> 30 μg Ethinylestradiol
>
> and
>
> 150 μg Levonorgestrel
>
> *(21 beige tablets)*

Biphasic preparations are presented in a schedule of 21 days containing a fixed dosage of Ethinylestradiol with increased dosage of Norethisterone as shown in Figure 5.4. This is followed by seven days of no pill-taking.

Pre-teen and teenage pregnancy

Figure 5.4　　　　　**Presentation of the Biphasic COC – BiNovum**

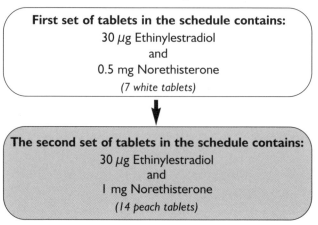

First set of tablets in the schedule contains:
30 μg Ethinylestradiol
and
0.5 mg Norethisterone
(7 white tablets)

The second set of tablets in the schedule contains:
30 μg Ethinylestradiol
and
1 mg Norethisterone
(14 peach tablets)

Triphasic preparations may contain varying amounts of Ethinylestradiol and progestogen in different forms for example Levonorgestrel or Norethisterone. One of the preparations in which the hormonal components vary in three different schedules is Trinordiol. This brand is presented as 21 or 28 days pills containing varied dosage of Ethinylestradiol with increasing dosage of Levonorgestrel as shown in Figure 5.5 below.

Figure 5.5　　　　　**Presentation of the Triphasic COC – Trinordiol**

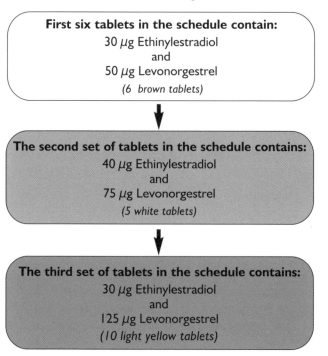

First six tablets in the schedule contain:
30 μg Ethinylestradiol
and
50 μg Levonorgestrel
(6 brown tablets)

The second set of tablets in the schedule contains:
40 μg Ethinylestradiol
and
75 μg Levonorgestrel
(5 white tablets)

The third set of tablets in the schedule contains:
30 μg Ethinylestradiol
and
125 μg Levonorgestrel
(10 light yellow tablets)

Contraceptive prescribing for young people

Pharmacologic effects of the hormone components of COC

The hormonal content of the monophasic COCs typically consists of oestrogens and progestogen in synthetic preparations at fixed dosages. The oestrogens in the forms of Ethinylestradiol in the current low dose preparations range from 20 to 35 micrograms. However, the progestogen component may differ in different monophasic preparations and the different synthetic forms include Norethisterone, Levonorgestrel and Norgestimate. The dosage of progestogen as indicated in the monophasic preparation – Microgynon shown in Figure 5.3 – is a relatively low 150 micrograms. Whichever the preparation of monophasic COC, the dosages of the oestrogen and progestogen remain constant in all the tablets (IPPF, 2002).

The hormonal content of the biphasic combined oral contraceptives is characteristically made up of different combinations of the oestrogen and progestogen in varying amounts. The modifications in the amount of hormone administered in any given preparation are designed to mimic the hormone variations in the first and second halves of the menstrual cycle. The example shown in Figure 5.4 (BiNovum) contains Ethinylestradiol at a fixed amount and increased dosage of Norethisterone.

Similarly to the biphasic COC, the triphasic preparations may contain different forms of the synthetic oestrogen and progestogen. These are designed to bring about cyclical effects as near as possible to the effects of the ovarian hormones produced in the natural menstrual cycle. Triphasic preparations may contain Ethinylestradiol at a constant dosage. However, other preparations such as the Trinordiol indicated in Figure 5.5 contain Ethinylestradiol at varying dosages of 30, 40 and 30 micrograms with Levonorgestrel at increasing dosages. The purpose of the hormone variations is to mimic the cyclical endometrial changes in the different phases of the natural menstrual cycle although this claim has not been substantiated strongly enough through research studies (IPPF, 2002; Guillebaud, 2000). The following section outlines the pharmacokinetics and bioavailability of the hormones.

Related pharmacokinetics implications

Various researchers have presented explanations of the interactions that occur in the absorption, metabolism, distribution and elimination of COC. Consistent evidence indicates that the absorption of Ethinylestradiol and progestogens occurs in the small intestine. Therefore, disruption of the process of absorption inevitably reduces the bioavailability and thus the desired clinical effect of the hormones. Vomiting occurring less than two hours following intake of COC may also have an indirect effect on the absorption of the hormones (Elliman, 2000; FFPRHC, 2005).

Following absorption the Ethinylestradiol and progestogens are carried through the circulatory system to the liver. However, other evidence also indicates that extensive first-pass metabolism of the Ethinylestradiol and progestogens in COC occurs in the small intestines and the liver. As a result the bioavailability of Ethinylestradiol is reduced to approximately 40 to 50% whilst that of progestogens may vary. The serum levels of both the Ethinylestradiol and the Levonorgestrel are estimated to reach a peak within one to four hours of ingestion. The transportation of Ethinylestradiol through the blood involves being bound to plasma albumin as well as the augmentation of the binding capacity of Sex Hormone Binding Globulin (SHBG). The Levonorgestrel is transported through the blood by being extensively bound to SHBG as well as plasma albumin (Elliman, 2000; FFPRHC, 2005).

The metabolism of Ethinylestradiol in the intestine and the liver results in the formation of sulphate and glucuronide conjugates. One of the key hepatic enzymes – cytochrome – accelerates the metabolism of Ethinylestradiol. This reduces the circulating concentration of Ethinylestradiol and progestogens and therefore the clinical effect of those contraceptive hormones.

Following the intestinal and liver metabolism, the conjugates and unaltered forms of Ethinylestradiol and progestogens are excreted into the small intestine. The conjugates are then broken down in the large intestine by hydrolytic enzymes released by bacteria in the large intestine into free metabolites which are reabsorbed and excreted in the urine. The progestogens that are not metabolised in that way are excreted in the faeces. Findings show that the degree of reabsorption and the rates of metabolic clearance of the contraceptive hormones vary widely among different women (Elliman, 2000; FFPRHC, 2005). Steroid hormones tend to be particularly poorly metabolised by people with impaired liver function.

In addition to these processes, the Glucose Tolerance Test (GTT) may be affected by COCs, resulting in raised Fasting Blood Sugar levels. Where there are concerns about the potential effects of these changes the relevant laboratory tests are repeated one to two months after the discontinuation of the COC. These findings do not suggest any association with population differences such as age, social background or race.

The findings highlighted in this section should raise the practitioner's awareness of the need for careful consideration to be given to the prescribing or injudicious support of client requests for combined oral contraceptives. The potential benefits are examined below, followed by an overview of the main advantages and disadvantages.

Interaction with other medications

Considering the complexity of the processes of absorption, metabolism, distribution and serum levels, and the systems by which the metabolites of Ethinylestradiol and Levonorgestrel are eliminated, COCs invariably interact with certain medications. Interaction with medications known as liver enzyme inducers accelerate oestrogen and progestogen metabolism resulting in reduced efficacy of the oral hormonal contraceptives. The main implications include:

- possible contraceptive failure
- the binding sites, in particular albumin protein, become limited because of increased demand
- the enterohepatic circulation of oestrogens can also become diminished (Guillebaud, 2000)
- breakthrough bleeding is not uncommon, particularly when COC is used concurrently with medications such as Rifampicin and Griseofulvin and other broad-spectrum antibiotics including Ampicillin and Tetracyclines. Therefore, adolescents who are taking prescribed antibiotics for acne would need to be considered with caution. A more acceptable alternative might be use of non-hormonal methods of contraception (BNF, 2005)
- the effect of broad-spectrum antibiotics in reducing the bacterial flora of the large intestine results in disruption of the enterohepatic circulation thus affecting the efficacy and effectiveness of oral contraceptives
- reduced glucose tolerance with increased need for insulin has also been reported among diabetic women who are prescribed combined oral contraceptives.

Pre-teen and teenage pregnancy

Summary of drug interactions

Anti-epileptic Drugs

- Phenytoin
- Carbamazepine
- Phenobarbital
- Primidone

Broad-spectrum Antibiotics

- Rifampicin
- Griseofulvin
- Ampicillin
- Tetracyclines

Whilst some of these are liver enzyme-inducing drugs others have the effect of impairing the bacterial flora which act on the conjugated Ethinylestradiol to achieve the enterohepatic circulation (BNA, 2005; FFPRHC, 2005).

Table 5.2   **Indications and Contra-indications**

Main Indications

- maximum protection from pregnancy
- preference for a contraceptive method that is independent of sexual intercourse

Non-contraceptive benefits
- treatment of primary dysmenorrhoea
- endometriosis
- dysfunctional uterine bleeding

For treatment of certain persistent gynaecological conditions even though contraception may not be required:
- menorrhagia
- Pre-Menstrual Syndrome
- functional ovarian cysts
- polycystic ovarian syndrome (PCOS) mainly to control the main symptoms
- following an ectopic pregnancy as HRT for young women who develop premature menopause

Absolute contra-indications

WHO categories:
i. no restriction to use of combined oral contraceptives
ii. advantages outweigh theoretical/ proven risks
iii. theoretical/proven risks outweigh the advantages but can be used with caution and additional care as a method of last choice
iv. condition represents unacceptable health risk and combined oral contraceptives should not be used

WHO category iv:
- pregnancy
- past or present circulatory disorders including: arterial or venus thromboembolis or ischaemic heart disease e.g. angina cardiomyopathy
- severe migraine
- transient ischaemic attacks with or without headaches
- high cholesterol > 8mmol/l
- blood dyscrasias
- auto-immune disorders
- elective major leg surgery
- during leg immobilisation
- during varicose vein treatment
- moderate to severe hypertension
- severe liver disorders including:
    - active liver disease with abnormal LFTs
    - viral and non-viral hepatitis and jaundice
- significant structural heart disease such as:
    - persistent septal defects
    - complex valve pathology
    - pulmonary hypertension
- current or history of epilepsy
- past acute pancreatitis
- trophoblastic disease requirement
- undiagnosed vaginal bleeding
- endometrial hyperplasia

Relative contra-indications and special precautions

- severe depression
- amenorrhoea/oligomenorrhoea
- high blood pressure
- long-term drug therapy
- chronic systemic disease – Crohn's disease
- coeliac disease – disorders of absorption

Intercurrent disease
- asthma
- multiple sclerosis
- Raynauds Disease
- Thyrotoxicosis
- renal disease
- cancer of colon
- Thalassaemia Major
- if risk of the pregnancy may cause deterioration of an existing medical condition
- conditions treated with drugs that interact with COCs
- Sickle Cell Disease

COC is associated with risk of thromboembolic disorders therefore, if taken by clients with sickle cell (SS or SC) disease a crisis with arterial stasis could exacerbate the risk of thrombosis. Anoxia and infections are conditions that could trigger an onset of a crisis.

- Diabetes mellitus

COC may affect glucose tolerance resulting in increased insulin.

Pre-teen and teenage pregnancy

Main aspects of client care, support and guidance

Taking account of the issues outlined above, the practitioner is faced with the responsibility of ensuring that the client is suitable for using combined oral contraceptive as the method of choice. Of equal importance, the practitioner needs to establish the individual's motivation to take the pills conscientiously in order to achieve the desired effectiveness without accidental pregnancy due to failed compliance. The following are the main considerations in the history and examination associated with the pill-taking.

Detailed history

Personal and family history should be carefully obtained to establish whether cardiovascular risk factors exist in the client's personal health or family members. A full medical history should include details of both previous and current medical conditions to establish any contraindications. The gynaecological and obstetric history should also include details of the menstrual history.

Any headaches should be thoroughly explored to find out the nature of attacks. In particular, the practitioner should determine details of how frequent, which side, when, how severe and whether there is an association with the menstrual cycle. It is also important to find out what factors usually trigger the onset of the headaches and what medications the individual takes to relieve the symptoms. The family history should establish the presence of any cardiovascular diseases such as hypertension, thrombosis and breast cancer. History of sexually transmitted infections, HIV status and Hepatitis B should also include information about any drug treatments that have been prescribed for these.

Physical examination

A thorough physical examination should be carried out particularly at the initial visit to the contraceptive clinic, prior to starting the contraceptive pill and at regular intervals as necessary. This should be performed prior to a discussion about the choice of contraceptive method. It is important that the information obtained is used effectively in providing the necessary explanations about the suitability or otherwise of the combined contraceptive method.

The baseline measures of weight and height are usually taken and BMI assessed. A cervical smear should be taken to exclude abnormal cell changes. Breast examination should be performed carefully using the correct technique but self breast awareness should also form part of the client education that is provided at that initial visit (Guillebaud, 2000).

Many people are likely to have heard about the risk of breast cancer that may be associated with use of combined oral contraceptive preparations and may have a serious concern. As Guillebaud (2000) and many experts suggest, this sensitive discussion should be dealt with carefully in a professional manner. Nevertheless, the discussion should form part of the routine interview and counselling provided. Practitioners are reminded to be tactful, particularly when addressing this issue with teenagers. Although this special client group tend not to be preoccupied by this risk, it is important nonetheless to provide them with appropriate education and encouragement to report any strange and abnormal sensations in the breasts, including any newly-observed changes.

The protective effects of the hormones include malignant disorders in the ovaries and the endometrium and these should also form part of the discussion. Many women will find that reassuring.

Points for consideration in prescribing combined oral contraceptives include:

- possibility of a drug interaction
- current medication including prescribed and non-prescription drugs and herbal drugs, e.g. St John's Wort
- client education and counselling – providing clear information about drugs that may reduce the effectiveness of hormonal contraceptives and the need for expert guidance, and
- advice on use of additional contraceptive methods or alternatives that are not affected by interaction with other drugs.

Instructions for taking COCs

The pill-taking instructions should be clear and concise to enhance recall and compliance. The main aspects of the instructions include the following:

- Tablets should be taken by mouth and the timing should be carefully considered to find the most suitable time of day to encourage consistency and compliance with the pill-taking routine. It should occur at the same time each day.

Pre-teen and teenage pregnancy

- The 21 day combined contraceptive tablets should be started on the first day of the cycle. At the end of the 21 days there is an interval of seven days when no pills are taken. Withdrawal bleeding occurs during that interval.
- If the starting date occurs later than the first day of the cycle, e.g. day four, it is important that additional method of contraception, such as the barrier method, is used for seven days (BNF, 2005).

The guidance on missed pills (Figure 5.6) reflects the latest WHO selected practice recommendations (SPR) update (2004).

Figure 5.6

Advice for women missing combined oral contraceptives (30–35 µg and 20 µg ethinylestradiol preparations)

If ONE or TWO 30–35 µg Ethinylestradiol pills have been missed at any time
OR
ONE 20 µg Ethinylestradiol pill is missed

If THREE or MORE 30–35 µg Ethinylestradiol pills have been missed at any time
OR
TWO or MORE 20 µg Ethinylestradiol pills are missed

The client should take the most recent missed pill as soon as she remembers.

She should continue taking the remaining pills daily at her usual time.*

She does not require additional contraceptive protection.

She does not require emergency contraception.

She should take the most recent missed pill as soon as she remembers.

She should continue taking the remaining pills daily at her usual time.*

She should be advised to use condoms or abstain from sex until she has taken pills for seven days in a row.

IN ADDITION
(because extending the pill-free interval is risky)

If pills are missed in week one (days 1–7)
(because the pill-free interval has been extended):

If pills are missed in week three (days 15–21)
(to avoid extending the pill-free interval):

emergency contraception should be considered if she had unprotected sex in the pill-free interval or in week one.

she should finish the pills in her current pack and start a new pack the next day, omitting the pill free interval.

* Depending on when she remembers her missed pill, she may take two pills on the same day (one at the moment of remembering and the other at the regular time) or even at the same time.

(FPA, 2005)

98

Contraceptive prescribing for young people

The WHO's recommendations are based on the principles that:

● the requirement to take an active hormonal contraceptive pill immediately when pills have been missed is crucial; and

● in those circumstances the possibility of pregnancy occurring depends on two key factors:

  – how many pills were missed, and

  – when the pills were missed.

The dosage of Ethinylestradiol in the particular COC preparation influences the chances of pregnancy in missed pills. Additionally, the timing during the cycle when the pills are missed is also crucial. For example, where three or more active hormonal pills are missed at any time during the cycle, or two or more 20 µg or less are missed, the recommendations suggest that extra contraceptive precautions should be used. This is because the risk is considered to be potentially higher with the missed 20 µg preparation than it is in the case of missed 30–35 µg preparations. Of particular importance is when the pills are missed – either at the beginning or at the end of the active pills, extending the pill-free interval. Therefore the inhibition of gonadotrophins and ovulation are crucial to the success of contraception.

Progestogen-only pill

Progestogen-only pill (POP)

Progestogen-only contraceptives may be used as an alternative form of oral hormonal contraception. Different preparations are available with varying amounts of the progestogen component as shown in Table 5.3 below.

Table 5.3

POP preparations and dosages

Preparation	Progestogen component	Schedule
Microval	Levonorgestrel 30 µg	35 days
Norgeston	Levonorgestrel 30 µg	35 days
Cerazette	Desogestrel 75 µg	28 days
Micronor	Norethisterone 350 µg	28 days
Noriday	Norethisterone 350 µg	28 days
Femulen	Etynodiol diacetate 500 µg	28 days

(BNF, 2005)

Pre-teen and teenage pregnancy

The mechanisms of action, pharmacologic effects and pharmaco-kinetic implications have been described above under hormonal contraceptives. In relation to the efficacy of POP, Guillebaud (2000) emphasises the importance of regular daily pill-taking irrespective of any bleeding patterns to achieve similar effects to the COC. Therefore, careful client education and correct instruction are very important.

The suggested starting routines depend on gynaecologic conditions. For example, in relation to the menstrual cycle the BNF (2005) recommends that POP be started on day one of the cycle and taken at the same time each day. However, post-natal women are advised to start on day 21 if not lactating. On the other hand, if full lactation has established the POP may be started anywhere from day 21 to 42 or later.

After a spontaneous or induced abortion, the recommendation is to start the POP on the same day (Guillebaud, 2000). Reduced contraceptive efficacy should be considered in the following situations:

● starting the pill-taking on day two of the cycle
● delayed pill-taking by a period longer than three hours
● vomiting or severe diarrhoea occurring within two hours after the pill has been taken
● missed pill.

In these situations additional contraceptive precaution is recommended for up to seven days. In cases of a missed pill the client is advised to take the pill as soon as she remembers but if missed for longer than three hours or 12 hours for Cerazette, then additional contraceptive precaution should be used for the next two days (BNF, 2005; FPA, 2006). However, if sexual intercourse occurs during the period of the missed pill, then emergency contraception should be considered.

Side-effects

The associated side-effects may vary in their manifestation and duration. Generally these tend to resolve in time but they can result in client discontinuation of the contraceptive method if they persist or if the client finds a particular problem to be distressing or difficult to cope with. Common side-effects include:

● menstrual irregularities

- breast discomfort
- nausea and vomiting
- headaches
- weight changes
- reduced libido
- skin disorders.

(BNF, 2005)

Table 5.4

Indications and contraindications of POP

Indications	Contraindications/ special precautions
Oestrogen-related problems e.g. history of venous thrombosis	Severe arterial disease
	Undiagnosed bleeding from the vagina
Women over 35 years of age	Possible pregnancy
Heavy smokers	Recent trophoblastic disease (until the urine and plasma values of hCG return to normal values)
Hypertension	
Heart disease	
Diabetes mellitus	Previous ectopic pregnancy
Post-natal lactating women	Liver adenoma or other existing liver disease
Migraine	
Menstrual irregularities	Functional ovarian cysts
Sickle Cell Disease	Sex steroid dependent cancer
Client preference	Enzyme-inducing medications

(Guillebaud, 2003; BNF, 2005)

Additionally, although the risk of breast cancer has been associated with oral hormonal contraceptives, some experts agree that further empirical studies are required. Nevertheless, attention should be paid to the Committee on the Safety of Medicine's advice that the small potential risk of breast cancer should be weighed against the benefits of POP (BNF, 2005).

Client education and advice

Similarly to the considerations addressed for COC prescription, client education for POP should include provision of accurate evidence-based information and instruction on correct pill-taking. Additionally, a detailed history and medical examination with follow-up care should form part of the client care considerations.

As Guillebaud suggests, forewarning the client about the possible minor side effects might increase the individual's tolerance of these during the initial stages until she is more stabilised on the POP (Guillebaud, as cited in Glasier and Gebbie (2000)).

Emergency contraception

Emergency contraception

In discussing the practical aspects of the different contraceptive methods consideration has to be given to the client problem situations where there is urgent need for intervention to prevent unwanted and unplanned pregnancies. The reality is that this problem is common among the sexually active population group of young people including under sixteens. The decision to resort to such measures should not be taken lightly. Multiple factors and implications have to be judiciously and sensitively considered and, where necessary, ongoing counselling support should form an important aspect of the care provision. The different methods of emergency contraception are designed to prevent pregnancy after unprotected sexual intercourse.

Common indications include:

● unanticipated sexual activity

● suspected failure of the contraceptive method being used, and

● sexual assault.

Circumstances requiring emergency contraception after failure of contraceptive methods

● COC 21 active pills – if three or more 30–35 µg ethinylestradiol pills or two or more 20 µg ethinylestradiol pills have been missed in the first week of pill taking (days one to seven) and unprotected sexual intercourse (UPSI) occurred in week one or the pill-free week.

● POP – if one or more POP pills have been missed or taken more than 3 hours late (more than 12 hours late for Cerazette) and UPSI occurred in the subsequent two days.

● IUCD – if complete or partial expulsion occurs or mid-cycle removal of an IUD/IUS is deemed necessary and UPSI has occurred in the last seven days.

● Progestogen-only injectables – if the contraceptive injection is late (longer than 14 weeks from the previous injection for medroxyprogesterone acetate or longer than ten weeks for norethisterone enentate) and UPSI has occurred.

- Barrier methods – if there has been failure of a barrier method.
- Use of liver-enzyme inducers – an additional barrier method is recommended if oral contraceptives, progestogen implants or contraceptive patch are taken concurrently with any liver-enzyme inducers (including St John's Wort). Also if there is UPSI or barrier method failure during, or in the 28 days following, use of liver-enzyme inducers.

(FFPRHC, 2006)

Hormonal emergency contraception

Preparations of oral hormonal emergency contraceptives

A combined form of hormonal emergency contraception referred to as the 'Yuzpe regime' contained oestrogens and progestogen. However, the more popular oral hormonal preparation in current use contains only progestogen without oestrogens and is thus referred to as Progestogen Only Emergency Contraception. The progestogen component is in the form of Levonorgestrel and its popularity seems to be related to the general finding that it is safer, more effective and causes fewer side effects (Family Education Trust, 2000). The current preparation, Levonelle-2, contains 750 micrograms of Levonorgestrel.

Regarding the pharmacokinetics of Levonorgestrel and the potential interactions with other medications there do not appear to be many significant findings. Nevertheless, some experts caution about the effects of liver-enzyme-nducing drugs similar to that of other oral hormonal contraceptives.

The modes of action

Although not clearly explained the main modes of action reported include:

- disruption of ovulation and
- prevention of implantation.

Recommended timing and efficacy

The timing for administering any emergency contraception is crucial if the desired effect of avoiding unwanted pregnancy is to be achieved. Research evidence indicates a success rate of 95% where the interval between the unprotected sexual intercourse and the start of the progestogen-only emergency contraceptive regime is less than 24 hours (Task Force on Postovulatory Methods of Fertility Regulation, 1998). The following is an outline of the main recommendations for use of the oral emergency contraceptive pill.

The ideal timing recommended is to start the regime for the Levonelle-2 progestogen-only emergency contraceptive as soon as possible to achieve a high degree of efficacy. However, administration could occur any time within 72 hours of unprotected sexual intercourse (FFPRHC, 2003; BNF, 2005).

The regime consists of two 750 microgram tablets to be taken as first dose repeated 12 to 16 hours later with a second dose of 750 micrograms. However, where poor client compliance is considered to be a possible risk that might compromise the efficacy of the Levonorgestrel a single total dose of 1500 micrograms (1.5 mg) is recommended (FFPRHC, 2003).

Client education and advice

Important issues to explain and discuss in emergency contraception are that a possible side effect may be nausea. If vomiting occurs within two hours, the client should be strongly advised to report to the clinic. The management may involve administration of anti-emetic with advice on use of an extra contraceptive in the form of a barrier method of contraception. Alternatively an emergency contraceptive intrauterine device may be inserted (FFPRHC, 2003).

It is also important to stress that emergency contraception does not prevent future pregnancy and so a reliable method of barrier contraception should be used conscientiously until the next menstrual cycle. Clients should also be made aware that the next menstrual cycle may occur earlier than expected or be slightly delayed. The importance of follow-up care should be explained and a pregnancy test may be carried out if the client reports a history of light, short or delayed period.

Emergency IUD

Emergency intrauterine contraceptive device

Insertion of an Intrauterine Contraceptive Device (ICD) may be a preferred choice of emergency contraception. Different types of copper-bearing intrauterine contraceptive devices are currently available. These include Flexi T-300, Multiload Cu-375, T-Safe 380 and Nova-T 380 (FFPRHC, 2003; Everett, 2005).

Contraceptive prescribing for young people

Modes of action, efficacy and timing

The efficacy of emergency intrauterine contraception depends on the timing of application following unprotected sexual intercourse which is considered to be critical for maximal performance. This method is considered to achieve a relatively higher rate of efficacy in preventing pregnancy because of its direct action on the endometrium. The main mode of action is prevention of implantation but other modes of action reported include:

- inhibition of sperm transport and prevention of fertilisation
- producing a process of foreign body reaction with increased leucocytes and phagocytes.

The recommended ideal timing for insertion is within five days (120 hours) of unprotected sexual intercourse or up to five days after the expected date of ovulation. However this could prove difficult for some clients to report accurately. Although insertion of intrauterine contraceptive devices is found to be easier at the end of menstruation, in reality sexual activity may occur at any time in the menstrual cycle and insertion may be required within an appropriate time to prevent pregnancy.

Clinical considerations

Despite the advantages, such as not being associated with drug interactions, a careful history should be obtained together with client interviewing and counselling. The aim is to ensure client safety and to enhance the efficacy of the method. Among the contraindications previously outlined for COC, Table 5.5 shows factors that should be carefully considered as contraindications, for the use of an emergency ICD.

Table 5.5

Contraindications for the use of an emergency IUD

Absolute contraindications	Relative contraindications
Current pregnancy	Previous pelvic infection
Previous ectopic pregnancy	Uterine fibroids
Uterine abnormalities	Nulliparous woman
Current genital tract infections	Diabetes mellitus
Undiagnosed genital tract bleeding	Dysmenorrhoea and menorrhagia

A pre-insertion pelvic examination may be carried out to establish the uterine position and normality and to exclude unusual tenderness which may indicate pelvic infection.

Client education and support

The main issues that need to be explained to the client include the risk of pelvic infection that could occur during the first 20 days of insertion of the intrauterine device. This is thought to be usually related to an existing STD and so screening is crucial, and a common practice is to screen for chlamydia and trichomonas infections prior to insertion being performed. The related symptoms should be explained and the client encouraged to report at the clinic without delay if she experiences any of the symptoms. Clients who fall into the high risk category for STDs should be tested before insertion of the intrauterine device. Some experts recommend prophylactic antibiotics as a routine at the insertion of an emergency intrauterine contraceptive (FFPRHC, 2003).

The procedure may be rather daunting for the client and careful explanations may help to reduce the anxiety and nervousness of many clients. It may help to reassure them that the procedure will be carried out gently to try and minimise discomfort. It may also reassure her that the device could be removed if necessary, but that other reliable forms of contraception would need to be used if pregnancy is to be avoided.

Following insertion, the client should be instructed on how to check the threads to ensure that the device is in place. Education and information should include awareness of the potential complications such as:

● exacerbation of pelvic infection

● uterine perforation

● ectopic pregnancy

● pain and consistent bleeding.

Additionally, she should be made aware of the importance of follow-up within four to six weeks following insertion, to assess the status of the IUCD and client satisfaction. Strong advice should be given to report to the clinic without delay for medical aid if any problems including persistent pelvic pain are experienced (BNA, 2005; Everett, 2005).

Intrauterine progestogen device

Intrauterine progestogen device

This type of intrauterine contraceptive method is referred to as Levonorgestrel intrauterine system. The Levonorgestrel is released at a dosage of 20 micrograms per day and the rate of efficacy and effectiveness are comparable to those of the other intrauterine contraceptive methods, although side effects are fewer and the risk of ectopic pregnancy is greatly reduced.

Modes of action, advantages and disadvantages

These are also similar to other intrauterine methods, the direct effect on the endometrium preventing the normal proliferative changes that occur in the normal menstrual cycle. Other effects include suppression of ovulation, thickening of the cervical mucus and changes in the uterine tubes.

The main advantages include the high effectiveness, improvement in dysmenorrhoea and reduced risk of pelvic inflammatory disease. On the other hand, disadvantages include abnormal patterns of bleeding such as intermenstrual bleeding and amenorrhoea. Some reported side effects include abdominal pain, peripheral oedema and migraine (BNF, 2005).

Clinical considerations

The recommended timing for insertion into the uterine cavity is within seven days of the onset of the menstrual cycle. Client care and support and follow up are similar to those previously discussed for other intrauterine contraceptive methods.

Progestogen-only injectable contraceptives

Progestogen injectable contraceptive

Injectable contraceptives are preferred by some clients because of the main advantage of not being related to sexual intercourse. They are also found to be suitable for women who suffer from premenstrual syndrome, dysmenorrhoea and menorrhagia, endometriosis and sickle cell disease.

Depo-Provera

Two different preparations are available. Depo-Provera consists of 150 mg of Medroxyprogesterone Acetate (DMPA). This is administered by deep intramuscular injection every three months and is described as having a similar rate of efficacy as the combined oral contraceptives. However, because of its long-term effect, careful client information and counselling are recommended for the following reasons:

- irregular cycles
- risk of heavy and/or prolonged bleeding in the immediate postpartum period
- delayed return of normal fertility.

A rare complication that has been reported is reduced mineral bone density and osteoporosis in the first two to three years of consistent use of this method. Therefore, the current recommendation is to use this only selectively for adolescents if other methods of contraception are not suitable for them. It is also recommended that this injectable contraceptive should be discontinued after two years and not used for individuals who may be at risk of osteoporosis (BNF, 2005). The main recommendation is that it should be administered within five days of the beginning of the menstrual cycle.

Noristerat

This type of injectable contraceptive is also a long-acting progestogen which consists of 200 mg of Norethisterone enantate in an oily preparation. This preparation is administered by deep intramuscular injection and is reported to provide contraception for up to eight weeks. The main advantages reported are that its mode of action of inhibiting ovulation protects against ectopic pregnancy and ovarian cysts. The related contraindications are found to be similar to those of the combined hormonal oral contraceptives (BNF, 2005).

Clinical considerations

The clinical considerations are similar in both types of injectable contraceptives. Important aspects of care include:

- obtaining a detailed medical history to exclude contraindications
- weight and blood pressure recordings.

As part of the client education and counselling, smoking habits should be explored and appropriate advice provided. Additionally, breast awareness should be addressed.

The main interactions that have been reported with other medications are liver-enzyme-inducing drugs (IPPF, 2002; Everett, 2005).

Progestogen-only implants

Progestogen implants

This method of contraception involves a sub-dermal insertion of a capsule which releases etonogestrel into the body. It is described as a medium to long-term contraception. The current preparation available in the UK is Implanon. This preparation is reported to have a lifespan of three years (IPPF, 2002; Everett, 2005).

Timing and rate of efficacy

A high rate of effectiveness is reported as being approximately 100% which is partly attributable to not being reliant on client compliance. The recommended timing for insertion is the first day of the menstrual cycle to achieve immediate effect or during the first five days. The modes of action are reported as:

● prevention of ovulation
● thickening of the cervical mucus which inhibits sperm transportation and
● changes in the endometrium (IPPF, 2002; Everett, 2005).

All of these are similar to those of other hormonal methods previously reported.

Client care considerations

Some side effects reported in relation to implants include bleeding problems and disruption of or irregular menstrual cycles. The incidence of amenorrhoea is found to increase with prolonged use. Therefore, client education and counselling should form an important aspect of the client care and support.

In terms of drug interactions, Rifampicin and Griseofulvin as well as the anticonvulsants Phenytoin and Carbamazepine and barbiturates have been reported as reducing the effectiveness of the contraceptive implants. The importance of follow-up should be emphasised, as in the case of all other hormonal contraceptives (IPPF, 2002; Everett, 2005).

Pre-teen and teenage pregnancy

Vaginal contraceptive rings (CVR)

Vaginal rings

This form of contraception is considered as being safe and convenient. Efficacy has been rated as being comparable to the combined oral contraceptive pill. Therefore, the failure rate is claimed to be one out of 100 women using the CVR. The product, which is referred to as NuvaRing, consists of a flexible transparent ring of plastic material (polysiloxone) 5.5 cm in diameter. The hormonal component may be a combination of progestogen in the form of Levonorgestrel plus oestrogens in the form of oestradiol or only progestogen. Various clinical trials have been conducted to test the Levonorgestrel-releasing-only CVR and trials on the combined preparations have also been conducted with varied results about the efficacy and continued use by women (Mishell, 1993).

Administration and client education

The ring is inserted into the vagina where it is left in place constantly for 21 days. The first day of insertion may be day one to five of the menstrual cycle. The mechanism involves slow release of the hormone component which absorbs through the wall of the vagina into the circulatory system. Client education and instruction are crucial to ensure correct use to achieve the desired effect (IFPA, 2007). Removal of the CVR at the end of the three weeks should also be emphasised. A period of seven days with no CVR in situ allows bleeding to occur. This should be explained to the client to avoid undue anxiety. Another crucial aspect emphasised in the client instruction is the importance of using extra contraceptive precaution in the first seven days of the first month.

Factors affecting the efficacy of CVR

- If the client forgets to insert a new ring at the end of the seven day break, the importance of not delaying to insert a new ring as soon as she remembers should be emphasised. The client should be made aware of the potential implication of the risk of pregnancy with prolonged delays. She should be instructed to insert a new CVR immediately and encouraged to use an extra contraceptive method, such as condoms, for the next seven days.
- If the CVR is left in situ for longer than 21 days, up to 28 days, the client should be instructed to remove the ring, allow the seven days break and insert a new CVR without delay.

- After 28 days the contraceptive protection of the retained ring would be considerably reduced. Therefore, the client should be instructed to remove the ring and seek further advice at the family planning clinic. If she has engaged in unprotected sexual intercourse during that period then the healthcare professional may suggest that a pregnancy test be carried out and emergency contraceptive method prescribed if pregnancy is not desired.

(IFPA, 2007)

Clients should be made aware that this method of contraception would not provide protection against STDs. Appropriate sexual health relationships education should be designed to specifically address STDs for the population group of young people.

Side-effects

It is the duty of the healthcare professional to raise the client's awareness of possible side-effects which are similar to those associated with the COC. They include:

- nausea
- breast tenderness
- mood swings
- headaches
- abnormal bleeding problems
- weight changes, and
- increased vaginal discharge, discomfort and irritation have also been reported by users of CVR.

Although found to be rare, serious complications similar to those associated with the COC have also been reported (University of Oregon, 2005; IFPA, 2007).

The contraceptive patch (Evra)

Contraceptive patch

This method of contraception consists of a beige coloured patch about 5 cm by 5 cm in size with hormone components of oestrogens and progestogen similar to the COC. Its effectiveness is rated as 99% if correctly applied. Reduced effectiveness is also associated with obesity – women who weigh 90kg or more (FPA, 2006).

Application of the contraceptive patch

Although the actual timing of starting the patch is not restricted to any particular day of the menstrual cycle, immediate protection is more likely to be achieved if started from the first day of the cycle. This is also possible up to day five of the cycle. Nonetheless, this method of contraception may be started on any day of the menstrual cycle. It is crucial, however, that pregnancy has not occurred already prior to commencement of the method. Women who have shorter cycles of 23 days, for example, should be advised to start using the method from day one to achieve immediate protection otherwise they should be advised to use additional contraceptive protection (FPA, 2006).

Once the method is started a patch cycle should be established and simple instructions should be given to the client as follows.

- On the start day of week one a new patch is applied and kept on for seven days.
- On the first day of week two, i.e. at the end of the first seven days, the first patch is discarded and a new patch applied right away and left in place for seven days.
- On the first day of week three, the patch from week two is discarded and a new patch applied right away. This is also left in place for seven days.
- At the end of week three, the used patch is discarded and a patch-free week allowed.
- After the seven patch-free days, a new patch cycle should be started without delay.

(FPA, 2006)

Careful advice should be provided regarding what actions to take if a patch becomes dislodged or lost, depending on how long since the patch became dislodged. If it is less than 48 hours, the client is advised to reapply the patch right away, if possible, but, if not, then a new patch should be applied to continue the normal patch cycle. If the patch has been off for 48 hours or longer then the recommendation is to commence a new patch cycle with a fresh pack right away in order to count that as the start day of week one. In addition, it is recommended that the client should be advised to use extra contraceptive protection for the next seven days.

The same process applies if the client forgets to remove and replace the previous patch. However, if removal of the patch is delayed at the end of week three then the client is advised to remove the old patch immediately but this may result in less than seven days patch free break in that cycle (FPA, 2006).

Patch use following abortion or childbirth

Although the patch can be started immediately after spontaneous or induced abortion at less than 24 weeks gestation, this differs for post-partum women. The timing may be delayed till 21 days post-partum if not breastfeeding. However, a breastfeeding woman may be advised to use other contraceptive methods to avoid disruption of her lactation (FPA, 2006).

The mode of action, indications and contraindications are reported to be similar to those of the COC method. Therefore, the same principles of client care considerations apply in terms of a detailed history, physical examination, client education and instructions on the use of the method. There is no doubt that specific advantages of this method may underpin the decision of many users who prefer this to other contraceptive methods.

Similarly to COC, the aspects of client care and support relating to drug interactions should be carefully considered. Additionally, longer periods without use of the patch may indicate a need for emergency contraception if the client has been engaging in unprotected sexual intercourse. Client education, clear instruction and support cannot be overemphasised in these situations.

Advantages and disadvantages

The main advantages are:

- application and use of the patch is unrelated to sexual intercourse and does not interrupt sexual activity
- the patch is unaffected by malabsorption problems
- it gives regulation of the menstrual cycle with less heavy and less painful periods
- it gives less severe premenstrual symptoms
- it may reduce the risk of ovarian and uterine cancers and functional ovarian cysts.

The main disadvantages are:

- depending on the site of application, the patch may be visible and may cause skin irritation

- the patch does not provide protection against STDs
- the patch has similar temporary side effects to the COC method.

(FPA, 2006)

Again, the healthcare professional is responsible for providing the same standard and quality of client care, education and support with follow-up care as is provided to the users of the COC method.

Patient Group Directions in sexual healthcare

Patient Group Directions

The importance of client safety and the impact of change in healthcare demands and societal expectations are emphasised in the code of professional conduct, policy guidelines and regulatory systems in place. Professional bodies, as well as the stakeholders and consumer representatives, expect high standards and quality of care and service provision to deal effectively with specific health issues according to the nature of demand.

Within the context of sexual and reproductive healthcare and service provision an ongoing concern relates to the high incidence of unplanned and unwanted pregnancies and STDs among adolescents and young adults. Various initiatives, strategies and proposals have evolved to establish possible ways of dealing with the problems realistically and effectively.

Patient Group Directions (PGDs) are currently implemented in many areas within the clinical care sectors and within the contexts of community care and service provision. The aim is to meet the increasingly changing demands and expectations by improving accessibility to a wide range of services, whilst acknowledging and empowering the identified groups of the health service users irrespective of age, gender or social backgrounds (DH, 1998).

The PGDs stipulate specific policies and guidelines which authorise appropriately-qualified practitioners to assess, diagnose and implement procedural interventions and treatments. Thus, for the extended role of qualified nurses with various specialist qualifications or additional certificates in Nurse Prescribing, PGDs are useful in professional practice. The terms and conditions of the PGD may authorise particular nurses to supply particular medications to identified patient groups without doctors' prescriptions (DH, 1998).

Contraceptive prescribing for young people

Within the context of sexual and reproductive healthcare provision, PGDs are increasingly in place to enable experienced family planning nurses to supply specific contraceptive methods including hormonal oral contraceptives. In some Health Board areas the PGDs are seen as a way of dealing with consistently high demands among the adolescent and young adult groups for emergency contraceptives.

Such nurses who function in sexual health clinics are required to have attained the relevant professional qualification and registration. Nurses operating at such levels are also expected to demonstrate awareness and a clear understanding of the following:

● NMC Code of Professional Conduct: Standards for Conduct, Performance and Ethics (2004)
● Guidelines for the Administration of Medicines (2004)
● Guidelines for Records and Record Keeping (2005).

The Health Boards may also stipulate that the nurses should:

● possess appropriate qualification(s)
● have attained additional specialist qualification where applicable
● undertake specific training
● have the required level of experience and competence relevant to the specific area of clinical practice, the specific clinical condition and the specific medication(s) used.

(Marshall *et al.*, 1997; Brittain, 1999)

Additionally, PGDs may stipulate that the qualified staff maintain their own level of competence through regular updates. They are also required to compile an annual record of evidence of all the training which they undertake.

Ethical and legal issues: under 16s and contraception

Ethical and legal issues

One of the main principles of medical ethics involves respect for an individual's decision about his or her own healthcare. It is important that a client understands all the information about her medical problem, what treatment options are available for that condition and consequences of declining to have the treatment. She should be considered capable of determining her choice of treatment if feasible.

This principle places a duty on the doctor to respect the client's confidentiality and not to divulge any detail about her to another person without her consent. The problem for the healthcare practitioner is knowing for certain whether the client, the young adolescent, is capable of making a decision about the particular treatment.

In the case of an adolescent girl, if it can be established that she understands the nature of the treatment that she requires and the potential consequences of keeping this from her parents and if she is emphatic that her parents should not be told, then the principle of respect for autonomy should apply and her confidentiality must be respected. However, other ethical considerations could work against respecting an adolescent's autonomous decision in a particular case. In some cases, in which complying with the request for confidentiality might have harmful consequences for herself or for others, a conflict of interest arises between best interest, maleficence and her right to autonomy.

The practitioner is faced with the challenge of having to weigh up the consequences of breaching, or not breaching, her confidentiality. Careful thought should also be given to the potential damage that could result. Any decision to breach confidentiality has to be seen to supersede her autonomy.

Beneficence versus confidentiality

In deciding what is in the best interest of the consulting adolescent girl, the practitioner should bear in mind that applying the principle of beneficence might not be a simple matter. If the practitioner claims to respect the adolescent's autonomous request for confidentiality then, in regard to the principle of beneficence, they still have a duty to ensure that everything possible is done to achieve a positive outcome for the girl. This should be discussed with her and any decisions to involve somebody else to provide emotional support for the girl must take account of her preference for a particular relative, friend or member of professional staff among the team of carers.

The related legislation

The legal situation varies across the UK. In relation to the legal age of consent within the English law, an individual patient or client is regarded as a minor until eighteen years of age. In Scotland, the

Contraceptive prescribing for young people

equivalent age is sixteen, whilst in Northern Ireland the age of sexual consent is seventeen, although the age of medical consent is sixteen.

The Family Law Reform Act England and Wales (1969) provides adolescents with a statutory right to consent to their personal medical treatment from the age of sixteen years. This means that consent to any surgical medical or dental treatment is just as legal and effective as in the case of adults. The law states that if a sixteen- or seventeen-year-old adolescent is considered to have given appropriately effective consent it is not necessary to obtain consent from a parent. An adolescent under sixteen years of age may consent to medical treatment, provided that he or she is deemed to have adequate intelligence and understanding to recognise the importance of the information and advice provided about the type of treatment.

The client should be able to demonstrate having adequately grasped what the specific treatment means and what it involves. This represents elements of the kind of common law used in Gillick vs West Norfolk and Wisbech AHA. That case deliberated a teenage girl's consent to be provided contraceptive advice without the knowledge or consent of her parents. The question arises as to what circumstances may justify a breach of the teenage client's confidentiality (DHSS, 1986).

As the healthcare professional's duty of confidentiality to adults falls into the contexts of both the legal and professional requirements, it could be argued that the same duty should be applicable to the pre-teen or adolescent who portrays adequate competence to consent to her own treatment without the need for parental consent.

The House of Lords rulings on Gillick vs West Norfolk and Wisbech AHA, contained three key elements:

A girl under sixteen of sufficient understanding and intelligence may have the legal capacity to give valid consent to contraceptive advice and treatment including necessary medical examination.

Giving such advice and treatment to a girl under sixteen without parental consent does not necessarily infringe parental rights.

Doctors giving such advice in good faith are not committing a criminal offence of aiding and abetting unlawful intercourse with girls under sixteen.

(DH, 2004)

Pre-teen and teenage pregnancy

Interpretation of the guidelines for practical application

The above extract comes from a recent review of these issues in relation to consent, confidentiality and autonomy for teenage girls seeking terminations published by the Department of Health (DH, 2004). The following summary outlines and expands on certain aspects of the key points in that guidance, which was derived from the House of Lords ruling, now commonly referred to as the Fraser guidelines.

Despite the emphasis on respecting the young adolescent's confidentiality, autonomy and consent, health professionals are also advised to try to avoid undermining parental responsibility and family stability. Therefore, the guidelines stress once again the importance of persuading the young person to tell her parents or guardian or other responsible person in her life. Alternatively the doctor or health professional may try to persuade the girl to allow them to inform the parents that advice or treatment has been or needs to be given. But where there has been a breakdown of family relationship, or for some other reason, it may not be possible to persuade the young person either to inform the parents or to allow the doctor or health professional to do so. In such cases there would be justification for giving advice and treatment without parental knowledge or consent provided that the professional satisfies himself or herself:

> That the young person could understand his advice and had sufficient maturity to understand what was involved in terms of the moral, social and emotional implications;

> That he could neither persuade the young person to inform the parents nor allow him to inform them that contraception advice was being sought;

> That the young person would be very likely to begin or continue having, sexual intercourse with or without contraceptive treatment;

> That without contraceptive advice or treatment the young person's physical or mental health, or both, would be likely to suffer;

> That the young person's best interests required him to give contraceptive advice, treatment or both without parental consent.

(DH, 2004)

Contraceptive prescribing for young people

The above decisions are left to the discretion of the doctor or health professional. In that context, if a doctor who is not the young person's primary physician considers that it is in the best interest of the adolescent to prescribe contraception without parental consent, then they are urged to obtain the client's consent for contacting her primary physician. This enables the doctor or other health professional to discuss the matter confidentially, with him or her, before making his decision to provide the treatment (FPA, 2005).

This guideline is particularly important since it may also provide an opportunity to find out whether there are any significant contraindications for the use of particular contraceptive methods. Should that be the case, the identified method may have to be provided with consideration to any related precautions or an alternative type of contraceptive treatment be prescribed.

An increasingly popular idea in setting up contraceptive services for young people is the notion of teenage-specific clinics in informal and user-friendly environments to reduce anxiety and nervousness. More importantly the aim is to encourage young people's attendance and engagement in the various health education activities. In these separate and less formal set-ups, an important consideration should be that staff are experienced in dealing sensitively with young people and their problems.

Guidelines provided by the statutory professional bodies

The British Medical Association (BMA) and the Royal College of General Practitioners (RCGP) provide regular updates on the guidelines relating to doctors to highlight emerging legislation and ethical debates relating to the under sixteens. A guidance statement by the BMA regarding inability to obtain parental consent advises the doctor to decide:

> Whether the girl has the mental maturity to understand the possible consequences of her action. If she has not, then her consent is not informed and so invalid. If he is satisfied that she can consent, he makes a clinical decision as to whether the provision of contraception is in the best interests of the patient. A decision not to prescribe does not absolve him from keeping the interview confidential.
>
> (BMA, 1988)

Pre-teen and teenage pregnancy

The General Medical Council (GMC) advocates the principle that, where necessary, confidentiality could be breached if there is a risk that serious harm may occur as a consequence of not divulging in a particular patient or client situation. The GMC's guidance statement on disclosure of confidential information states:

> A doctor who decides to disclose confidential information about an individual must be prepared to explain and justify that decision, whatever the circumstances of the disclosure.
>
> (GMC, 1991)

Although similar guidelines are provided by the Nursing and Midwifery Council (NMC) and the Royal Colleges of Nursing and Midwifery, these require careful consideration in their own right. It may be necessary to seek further guidance for clarification when practitioners find themselves confronted with particular client situations within the contexts of care/service provision (NMC, 2004).

The government perspective

In their *Revised Guidance for Health Professionals on the Provision of Contraceptive Services for Under 16s* (DH, 2004), for the first time the Department of Health emphasises the need to pay regard to the request of under sixteens. It states that, in response to the request for contraception, health professionals should establish a sympathetic and compassionate relationship with the adolescent. They are also encouraged to provide the required support, time and appropriate information to enable the adolescent clients to make informed choices. This should be achieved through a discussion that takes account of the following issues.

1. The discussion should include explanation of the emotional and physical consequences of engaging in sexual intercourse. The risks associated with teen pregnancy and sexually transmitted infections should also be taken into account.

2. The discussion should take account of whether the relationship is mutually agreed or whether the young girl is in a situation of coercion or sexual abuse.

3. The benefits of informing her GP and encouraging discussion with a parent or carer should be explained to the adolescent girl to try and gain her consent. Nevertheless, the guidelines also stress that any refusal should be respected. In such cases, as in the case of abortion, where the young woman is competent to consent but

cannot be persuaded to involve a parent, every effort should be made to help her find another adult to provide the required support. This may be another family member or specialist youth worker.

4. Account should be taken of additional counselling or support needs which the girl may require.

(DH, 2004c)

Clearly the complexity of the problems relating to contraceptive prescribing for the under sixteens is well acknowledged. The range of initiatives, protocols and procedures that are in place indicate that the vulnerability of this client group continues to be addressed with concern for their health, welfare and interests.

Conclusion

The prescribing of contraceptives for young adolescents under sixteen remains controversial. Nevertheless, the Government plans to reduce the rate of teenage pregnancies throughout the country. In an attempt to achieve that aim, various policies and practices have been developed and implemented. As yet there are no substantial findings from research to suggest that specific contraceptive methods are particularly suitable for younger girls and so different regimes and protocols are employed in different NHS Health Board areas based on local policies.

In order to examine the pharmacologic properties of the different hormonal contraceptive methods, this chapter began with an overview of the physiology of the menstrual cycle. It went on to review the various contraceptive methods currently available, in terms of their modes of action, effectiveness, advantages and risks, to provide some insight into the factors that practitioners will need to take into account when prescribing hormonal contraceptives to under sixteens. The client's social context, as well as their medical and gynaecological history, will always need to be taken into account, along with a physical examination, interview and careful counselling. The vulnerability of young adolescents must be taken seriously and all these aspects should play a part in choosing appropriate prescriptions, education and support for this client group.

Pre-teen and teenage pregnancy

The final part of the chapter explored ongoing legal and ethical debates about the prescribing of contraceptives to the under sixteens. It also reviewed the current guidelines for doctors and other health professionals relating to the rights, consent and confidentiality of young people. There appears to be consensus that the provision of contraception to under sixteens is an important but complex area, on which further training for professionals and education for young people is required.

References

British Medical Association (1988) *Philosophy and Practice of Medical Ethics* London: BMA.

British Medical Journal Publishing Group & Royal Pharmaceutical Society of Great Britain (2005) *British National Formulary* London: BMJ & RPS.

Brittain, D. (1999) Establishing an educational programme for nurses to supply emergency contraception (combined method) to protocol. *British Journal of Family Planning* 25: 118–129.

Cull, P. (1989) (ed.) *The Sourcebook of Medical Illustration* Carnforth: Parthenon Publishing Group.

DH (1998) *Review of Prescribing, Supply and Administration of Medicines: A report on the supply and administration of medicines under group protocols.* London: DH.

DH (2004a) *Best Practice Guidance for Doctors and other Health Professionals on the Provision of Advice and Treatment to Young People Under 16 on Contraception, Sexual and Reproductive Health.*
Available at http://www.dh.gov.uk/PolicyAndGuidance.

DH (2004b) *Publication of Revised Guidance for Health Professionals on the Provision of Contraceptive Services for Under 16s.*
Available at http://www.dh.gov.uk/Publicationsandstatistics.

DH (2004c) The *NHS Knowledge and Skills Framework and the Development Process* London: DH.

DHSS (1986) *Family Planning Services for Young People* London: DHSS.

Drugs Direct (2007) *What are the Types of Hormonal Contraception?*
Available at http://www.drugdigest.org/DD/HC.

Elliman, A. (2000) Interactions with hormonal contraception. *Journal of Family Planning and Reproductive Health Care* 26: 109–111.

Everett, S. (2005) Contraception. In Andrews, G. (ed.) *Women's Sexual Health* 4th edn. Edinburgh: Elsevier.

Faculty of Family Planning and Reproduction Health Care (2003) FFPRHC Guidance Emergency Contraception. *Journal of Family Planning and Reproductive Health Care* 29(2): 9–16.

Faculty of Family Planning and Reproduction Health Care (2005) *Faculty Statement from Clinical Effectiveness Unit on WHO Selected Practice Recommendations Update: Missed Pills – New recommendations.* Aberdeen: FFPRHC, the University of Aberdeen & Scottish Programme for Clinical Effectiveness in Reproductive Health. Available at http://www.ffrhe.org.uk (accessed May 2007).

Family Education Trust (2000) *Facing the Facts...Young People and the Morning-After Pill* London: The Family Education Trust.

Family Planning Association (2005) *The Legal Position Regarding Contraceptive Advice and Provision to Young People* FPA Factsheet. Belfast: FPA.

Pre-teen and teenage pregnancy

Family Planning Association (2006) *Information: Sexual health information service.* Available at http://www.fpa.org.uk/information.

General Medical Council (1991) *Guidance for Doctors on Professional Confidence* London: GMC.

Guillebaud, J. (2000) Combined hormonal contraception. In Glasier, A. and Gebbie, A. *Handbook of Family Planning and Reproductive Health Care* 4th edn. Edinburgh: Churchill Livingstone.

Guillebaud, J. (2004) *The Pill and Other Forms of Contraception: The facts* Edinburgh: Churchill Livingstone.

Irish Family Planning Association (2007) *Guide to Contraception: NuvaRing.* Available at http://www.ifpa.ie/contraception.nuv.htm1.

International Planned Parenthood Federation (2002) International Medical Advisory Panel Statement on Hormonal Methods of Contraception. *IPPF Medical Bulletin* 36(5): 1–8.

Kelly, G. (2003) *Sexuality Today: The human perspective* 7th edn. McGraw-Hill: New York.

Kumar, C. (1998) Contraceptive choices of women living in rural areas of Bihar. *British Journal of Family Planning* 24: 757.

Marshall, J., Edwards, C. and Lambert, M. (1997) Administration of medicines by emergency nurse practitioners according to protocols in an accident and emergency department. *Journal of Accident and Emergency Medicine* 14: 233–237.

Mishell, D.R. Jr. (1993) Vaginal contraceptive rings *Annals of Internal Medicine* 25(2): 191–197.

Nursing Midwifery Council (2004) *The PREP Handbook* London: NMC.

Steiner, M.J., Hertz-Picciotto, I., Raymond, E., Trussell, J., Wheeless, A. and Schoenbach, V. (1999) Influence of cycle variability and coital frequency on the risk of pregnancy. *Contraception* 60(3): 137–143.

Steiner, M.J. (1999) Contraceptive effectiveness: What should the counselling message be? *Journal of the American Medical Association* 282(15): 1405–1407.

Task Force on Postovulatory Methods of Fertility Regulation (1998) Randomised controlled trial of Levonorgestrel versus Yuzpe regimen of combined oral contraceptives for emergency contraception. *The Lancet* 352: 428–433.

University of Oregon (2005) *Vaginal Contraceptive Ring.* Available at http://healthcentre.uoregon.edu.

Wills, H. (2006) *Combined Oral Contraceptive.* Available at http://www.patient.co.uk.

World Health Organisation (2004) *Selected Practice Recommendations for Contraceptive Use.* 2nd edn. Geneva: WHO.

Chapter 6
Sex education in Scottish primary schools

Jason Annetts and Jan Law

The introduction of a comprehensive sex education curriculum in Scotland has been controversial (Dunphy, 2000; Lewis and Knijn, 2002), but it is vital if Scotland wishes to reduce its teenage pregnancy rates and reverse the rise in the incidence of sexually transmitted diseases (STDs) amongst young people. The experience of other European countries has demonstrated that the provision of a high quality and explicit programme of sex and relationships education (SRE) can provide young people with the necessary knowledge and skills to make informed choices and may help to reduce teenage pregnancy rates (Scottish Executive, 2000a; Health Scotland, 2006). Concern about sex education is most acute when it comes to primary school pupils, as it then becomes entangled with notions of childhood innocence and the fear of the further sexualisation of children (Epstein, 2000). However, the declining age of first sexual intercourse and the high rate of teenage pregnancies in Scotland relative to other parts of the UK and the EU has led healthcare practitioners and the Scottish Executive to recognise that sex and relationships education must begin in primary school (Scottish Executive, 2003).

In Scotland, unlike in England and Wales, there is no national curriculum and school governors do not need to approve a school's SRE programme. Although Scottish schools do now have to consult parents about the content of their sex education programmes, they are chiefly guided by local authorities and the Scottish Executive. The Executive's policy on the teaching of sex education in school has been outlined in a number of recent publications. Following the McCabe Report (Scottish Executive, 2000a), it published specific guidance on the content of the SRE curriculum to local authorities and schools (Scottish Executive, 2000b), as well as a leaflet for parents and carers outlining what their child would be taught (Scottish Executive, 2001). More recently, the Scottish Executive has published *Respect and Responsibility: Strategy and Action Plan for Improving Sexual Health*. This strategy is premised on the belief that 'sexual relationships are best delayed until a person is sufficiently mature to participate in a mutually respectful relationship' and that the purpose of sex and relationships education is 'to delay sexual activity' (Scottish Executive, 2005).

Respect and Responsibility puts schools and teachers at the centre of the sexual health strategy and emphasises the important role of teachers in improving the sexual health of young people in partnership with parents and health professions:

> Schools have a crucial part to play in fostering healthy attitudes towards relationships, sex and sexuality in young people. All schools are expected to provide sex and relationships education. High quality sex and relationships education should be delivered in an objective, balanced and sensitive manner by professionals who are trained for this role and who are able to support and complement the role of parents and carers as educators of children and young people.
>
> (Scottish Executive, 2005)

Respect and Responsibility reiterated the Scottish Executive's commitment to implementing the recommendations of the McCabe Report (Scottish Executive, 2000a) and recognised that improving young people's sexual health is in part dependent on the delivery of a successful sex and relationship programme to young people throughout their educational career. However, the Scottish Executive is unlikely to achieve its aims if delivery of the SRE curriculum is patchy and if teachers are not supported and appropriately trained for their new role as sexual health promoters.

The SHARE (Sexual Health and Relationship: Safe, Happy and Responsible) data seems to indicate that, in Scottish secondary schools at least, there is little consistency in either the time allocated to SRE or the content of the curriculum. Not only do these vary widely between local authorities and schools within a particular authority but even within individual schools (Buston *et al.*, 2001). Furthermore, the SHARE analysis clearly demonstrates that teachers find talking openly about sexual health and relationships 'difficult' but there is little in the way of support or training available.

There is no data on the delivery of SRE in Scottish primary schools but our research in Tayside would seem to suggest that, despite clear guidance from the Scottish Executive and the three Tayside local authorities, there is considerable variation between schools. While some is understandable, given the duty to consult with parents about the programme, it is largely the teachers and the head teacher who determine the actual content of the curriculum in a particular school. All children should have a right to good quality information on sex and relationships so that they can make informed choices and negotiate future sexual encounters effectively. Any differences in provision will mean that some children are less prepared and this may result in them having earlier sexual encounters, which evidence suggests that they are more likely to regret (Scottish Executive, 2000a; Wight and Henderson, 2004).

There is variability not simply in what is taught and what is not taught but also in the depth in which SRE topics are covered. The Scottish Executive rightly emphasises that topics in SRE should be taught in an appropriate way for the age and stage of the child, however, such vague guidance leaves the depth in which each topic is covered up to the judgement of the teacher and the school – a judgement that may be more influenced by how comfortable a teacher is with the material, the school policy and the demands of parents rather than the needs of the child.

One way in which this variability could be tackled is through a comprehensive training programme – such as Tayside Health Promotion's *Sexuality and Relationship Training for Primary School Teachers* – for teachers delivering SRE. The Scottish Executive has recognised the need to support teachers through both training provision and continuing professional development:

> Supporting teachers is key to the successful delivery of sex and relationships education, and the Executive is committed to ensuring that teachers receive appropriate training and continuing professional development, as well as knowledge about service delivery. Teachers will also benefit from being part of an integrated team delivering school-based sex and relationships education which receives clear policy direction regarding roles and responsibilities and whose work complements that of parents and carers, who will also be

informed and supported as educators in sex and relationships.

(Scottish Executive, 2005)

However, the extent to which this vision has actually been realised is unclear.

Evaluation of Sexuality and Relationship Training for Primary School Teachers

SRE evaluation

Although the Scottish Executive has emphasised the importance of delivering age-appropriate SRE throughout primary and secondary school, research in this area has tended to focus on sex education in secondary schools. There is no evaluative data for primary schools. This may be a reflection of the fact that a greater proportion of sex education is taught in secondary schools and an assumption that primary school children do not need it because of their sexual 'innocence'.

Clearly, the issue of childhood sexuality is controversial because of the widespread view that children should be sexually ignorant and 'that childhood should be devoid of sexuality' (Weis, 1999). However, a strong argument has been made that sex education should start in primary schools in order to provide 'positive information about sex and sexual health' (Scottish Executive, 2000a) and to prepare young people for the sexual health challenges that they will face in secondary schools (Wallis and Van Every, 2000). Despite the Scottish Executive's (2005) guidance to local authorities that SRE should be 'based on health guidelines and built upon throughout primary school as part of 5–14 health guidelines', we know very little about what is actually being taught and how this varies between schools and local authorities.

Tayside Health Promotion's *Sexuality and Relationship Training for Primary School Teachers* has been unique in its focus on primary school teachers. Working in collaboration with the three Tayside local authorities (Angus, Dundee and Perth & Kinross) for a decade, Tayside Health Promotion constructed a voluntary training programme for primary school teachers based upon the *Living and Growing* programme (Forrest, Souter and Walker 1994). As sexual health promotion becomes a formal aspect of teachers' role in primary schools, the establishment of such training will become a vital component ensuring consistency of delivery across

Sex education in Scottish primary schools

Scotland. Specific training on delivering the SRE curriculum is necessary to ensure that teachers have the requisite confidence and skills to become sexual health promoters in the classroom.

In 2004, the Scottish Executive funded a study to evaluate the success of Tayside Health Promotion's *Sexuality and Relationship Training for Primary School Teachers* in enabling teachers to become sexual health promoters in the classroom (Annetts and Law, 2006). Ensuring that teachers have both the skill and confidence to deliver SRE and promote positive images of sexuality is essential given that teachers and schools are at the very heart of the Scottish Executive's sexual health strategy. In accord with the aim of both *Enhancing Sexual Wellbeing in Scotland* (Scottish Executive, 2003) and *Respect and Responsibility* (Scottish Executive, 2005) this was an opportunity to evaluate the possible impact of such training programmes. A secondary aim was to map for the first time the provision of sex and relationships education in Tayside's primary schools.

The research was conducted between September 2004 and July 2006 and involved: a survey of head teachers in the 177 primary schools in the three Tayside local authorities; a pre-training question-naire and post-training interviews with teachers completing the *Sexuality and Relationship Training for Primary School Teachers* course during the 2004–5 school year; and interviews with teachers who had completed the training between 1996 and 2003.

The SRE curriculum

The SRE curriculum in Tayside's primary schools

As part of the Tayside research all 177 primary schools in the three Tayside local authorities were surveyed about the content of their SRE curriculum and the training, if any, teachers at the school had received. Of the 118 schools that completed this questionnaire, all either had, or were in the process of constructing, an SRE programme in accordance with the guidance given to them by their local authority and in consultation with parents. As recommended by Scottish Executive (Scottish Executive, 2000b; Scottish Executive, 2001), the majority of Tayside schools begin the SRE curriculum in either nursery or Primary 1 and involve all classroom teachers, embedding SRE topics throughout the school's curriculum. The primary focus of SRE in these early years is on family relationships and developing the children's understanding of their own bodies. Between Primary 5 and Primary 7, the majority of schools deal with the potentially more sensitive issues related to the onset of puberty and menstruation, changing nature of friendship and the development of sexual emotions, pregnancy and birth as well as responsible relationships.

This mapping exercise found that, although certain subjects – such as 'The Family and Other Special People that Care for Them', 'Being Part of a Family' and 'Dealing with a Bullying Situation' – were taught by nearly every school, no one topic was taught by all schools. Only two schools did not teach 'The Way Bodies Change and Grow' and three schools, rather surprisingly, did not teach 'The Family and Other Special People that Care for Them'. At the other end of the spectrum, the majority of schools (57%) did not include an 'awareness of sexually transmitted infections' in their SRE curriculum, while nearly half the schools did not cover parenting roles, contraception and family planning. The likely reason for this is a belief that primary school children do not need information on topics like sexually transmitted infections because they are not yet sexually active. The interviews with teachers conducted as part of the Tayside research also found that many teachers feel uncomfortable dealing with 'nitty-gritty' details of sexual relations and this may make them unwilling to discuss subjects such as contraception or sexually transmitted infections. This may be one of the reasons for the level of variation in the content of the SRE curriculum between schools. Perhaps one of the more surprising findings from the mapping exercise is that nearly 30% of schools surveyed did not teach 'permanent and responsible relationships' even though the Scottish Executive's guidance emphasises that schools should promote 'relationships based upon love and respect...the value of stable family life, including the responsibilities of parenthood and marriage' (Scottish Executive, 2001).

This level of variability was somewhat unexpected given that each Tayside local authority had recently rolled out an extensive SRE programme based around the *Living and Growing* videos. These programmes had also been supported in each local authority by a dedicated sexual health tutor and through their continued support of the *Sexuality and Relationship Training for Primary School Teachers* course. It is possible that the variation may simply reflect the different starting positions of schools in an area. For example, some schools already had a well established SRE programme prior to the implementation of the SRE curriculum, while others did not or were in the process of developing their SRE curriculum in consultation with parents. However, it would also appear that a school's SRE curriculum is influenced by how comfortable teachers at the school are with discussing sex and relationships with their pupils as well as what they consider to be necessary information.

Providing comprehensive training for teachers delivering SRE is likely to reduce the level of variation between schools. This is essential given that variability in the content of the SRE curriculum between different primary schools inevitably means that some children are receiving less information and have fewer opportunities to discuss sex and relationships than children in other schools. This would seem to be at odds with the current thinking that 'all children and young people are entitled to a balanced educational programme of sex and relationships education (SRE), which focuses on information provision, skills development and the clarification of attitudes and values' (Health Scotland, 2006).

Teachers and the delivery of SRE

Delivery of SRE

The mapping of SRE teaching in Tayside's primary schools has clearly shown that there is considerable variation in what is taught by different schools. The interviews with teachers further indicate that even within a school there is considerable variation in the delivery of the curriculum depending upon how comfortable a teacher is with the subject. Studies of sex and relationship teaching in secondary schools have demonstrated that many teachers feel uncomfortable discussing sexual issues with pupils (see Buston *et al.*, 2001) and this may reduce the effectiveness of the intervention (Scottish Executive, 2000a). However, the findings of the SHARE evaluation suggest teachers' discomfort may be reduced by training (Wight and Henderson, 2004).

Similarly, the Tayside research also found that participation in a training programme such as the Sexuality and Relationship Training for Primary School Teachers can alleviate the majority of teachers' concerns about the curriculum. Training increased teachers' confidence considerably in dealing with sexual subject matter and provided them with an opportunity to go through a programme before having to deliver it in the classroom:

I think that the big one, not just for me, but for everyone on the course, was the increased confidence. For me it was actually great getting out meeting other people and hearing about what is going on in other schools, sometimes you think my goodness we are not doing that, and other times when you hear what is happening, you think we are not quite so bad after all. You get both sides of the coin. But I think the big thing was the increased confidence and also just the time. Because you spent that time in the training, the time to go through the material, if somebody just gave you the package in the school and said there you go, make your way through that, you don't actually set aside time to go through everything and also the knowledge and experience of the people delivering the training, they were superb. It's just having that experience and knowledge you know if you gave a scenario, she came back at you, well here's how you might do this or you could try that. That was just so helpful to everyone. She had a way of dealing with things, nice and calm. (Head teacher, Angus)

Training, particularly external training, may also help to tackle the problem of variability. External training provides an opportunity for head teachers and teachers attending the training to evaluate their own programme in terms of what other schools are doing and in terms of the expectations of the Scottish Executive and their local authority. For example, one of the teachers interviewed felt that her colleagues were somewhat more conservative in what they felt was appropriate for pupils as part of the SRE curriculum and that attending the course confirmed her views and boosted her confidence:

Going on that course gave me the confidence. Because at the training we did in school I felt a wee bit out of step with everyone. People were sitting saying you know we shouldn't be doing that we shouldn't be watching that. I'd be watching that bit of the video but not that bit, and be tippexing clitoris out. My background was social work. I worked in children's units before where sex education is a huge issue, kids who are obviously active, and you realise how important it is, and I didn't have an issue with any of it, so I felt a wee bit of out of step, so it was really nice to go on this course. (Teacher, Primary 3–7, Dundee)

Sex education in Scottish primary schools

All the teachers interviewed as part of the evaluation recognised the need for the sex and relationship curriculum in primary schools, but, while the training boosted the confidence levels of teachers delivering the curriculum, several aspects of the *Living and Growing* videos and the SRE curriculum still caused them considerable unease. For example, there was considerable concern with aspects of the programmes that were considered too sexually explicit, the use of the word 'clitoris' and the discussion of homosexuality and contraception. Much of this concern stems from the teachers' own beliefs about what is appropriate knowledge for primary school children and it is this that may explain why some schools were happy providing information on contraception or discussing the issue of homosexuality while others were not.

Many of the teachers interviewed did not want to get into the 'nitty gritty' details of sexual relationships. For example, there was considerable disquiet about the cartoons depicting sexual intercourse in the *Living and Growing* programme:

> Possibly showing the children the actual sex act with cartoons is possibly something, maybe Primary 6 or 7. I don't think that it is all that necessary. They might know how it happens but I don't think they need to physically see the act... Now if that's in a TV programme what do you do? If the rest of the TV programme is fine. Even some of the cartoon bits are fine but some of it is not as necessary as they seem to think. I do want them to know how it happens, but I'm not sure about the actually physically showing the act. (Head teacher, Primary 1–3, Perth & Kinross)

Homosexuality

Similarly, while most teachers indicated that they were happy, if asked, explaining that homosexuality was when two members of the same sex loved one another, they did not feel it was appropriate to provide their pupils with any more details on gay relationships.

> We do deal with the two girls as partners, same sex relationships. Quite happy to discuss that is the path some people choose, not going into any nitty gritty, but I'm quite happy to discuss that it exists and they are classed as a couple the way

that a man and a woman are classed as a couple. They are in a loving caring relationship, I am quite happy to go down that line. (Depute Head Teacher, Dundee)

I think for me if one of the children asked me about it, I would answer it. Really just the same as anybody else in a consenting adult loving relationship the only difference being is it is of the same sex. I don't see anything wrong with that. But again it is a personal thing some people are really dead against. I wouldn't go into any of the nitty gritty what they did together, but I think if they ask then yes. (Teacher, Primary 5–6, Angus)

Once again the *Living and Growing* video was criticised, this time for showing unnecessary images of a gay male couple kissing. One school even felt it was necessary to edit out these images because of the head teacher's fear of Section 28 of the Local Government Act 1988, which forbade schools funded by local authorities to 'promote' homosexuality, even though Section 28 (or Section 2a of the Local Government Act 1986 as it was known in Scotland) was repealed by the Scottish Parliament in 2000. It is very surprising given the widespread publicity concerning the repeal of Section 2a, including the 'Keep the Clause' campaign, that a head teacher would not be aware that it was no longer on the statute books.

... *Living and Growing* videos are 98% good then you get this image that crosses the screen and you are left looking sideways thinking have I just seen what I thought I saw. And that's exactly what jarred for my parents when I showed them the Primary 5 material. They could just not quite take the two 'butch guys' kissing. (Head teacher, Dundee)

I did have a problem with the head teacher. She felt I think that the bill, Section 28, was making her a bit nervous and the bottom line was that the buck stops at her door, so she had to be happy with what was going on in her school and she wasn't happy about that, so that was cut out of the videos. (Depute head teacher, Dundee)

Given the scaremongering that has appeared in the media around what is actually being taught in schools about homosexuality and the furore that has been provoked by campaigns such as Brian's Souter's 'Keep the Clause' that sought to stop the Scottish Executive from repealing Section 2a, it is perhaps not surprising that teachers are worried about promoting positive images of gay couples. The heterosexist nature of schools as an institution has also been well documented (Buston and Hart, 2001) and therefore we should not be surprised that schools are reticent about discussing same sex relationships on an equal footing with heterosexual relationships. However, the danger of this is that schools can unintentionally promote homophobic attitudes which could result in some children being bullied. Although none of our interviewees had to deal with pupils who had self-identified as gay or lesbian, a number of teachers admitted that they had children in their classes who were being raised by a same sex couple and that for them it was important to discuss same sex relationships.

> Well I've had children in my class whose parents were of the same sex. And we have talked about these things, you have to talk about these things because for those children that's really important, that's their way of life and their friends know that. (Teacher, Primary 6, Dundee)

Contraction

Contraction

The discussion of contraception was another area that many teachers did not believe was particularly appropriate for primary school pupils. Like homosexuality, most teachers indicated that if they were asked a question they would answer it but not provide any detail.

> I didn't do much on contraception I must say … I try to sort of, I don't steer away from it. I mean if somebody asked me I would answer the question but I don't actually bring it up. As I say, I do mention that you know there are ways of avoiding pregnancies but then I also say, well, you're only ten and you shouldn't really be having sex until you're sixteen according to the law etc. so I bring a bit of law in as well so speak about ways and choices and that kind of thing. (Teacher, Primary 6–7, Angus)

> At this stage they shouldn't be thinking of conception therefore they shouldn't need the contraception. (Head teacher, Dundee)

Another teacher interviewed simply did not believe discussing issues such as contraception, homosexuality or sexually transmitted diseases was appropriate at primary school, at least not in any depth and, if information was required children should be directed to parents or maybe even to the young person's sexual health centre in Dundee, 'The Corner'.

> I have three things. I know the *Living and Growing* material touches on it, even just very briefly with a few seconds of footage. I don't believe that primary schools should be looking at contraception. I don't believe that we should be looking at homosexuality in depth and I don't believe that we should be looking at sexual transmitted diseases in detail … does it have to be in classrooms? Can this not be The Corner's work, where people elect to go for that information rather than well we were in the classroom and we just got it? (Head teacher, Dundee)

However, not all teachers interviewed agreed that contraception should not be taught in any detail. One teacher felt that much more needed to be done on contraception and that this was also the view of some of their parents because it was recognised that, by Primary 7, some pupils were becoming sexually active.

> Two parents stood up and said we can't close our eyes to the fact that children are having sex in Primary 7 whether we like it or not … They felt that more had to be in the programme about contraception, they didn't feel there was very much about that. I have to agree with that, I think more has to be in about contraception. We have taken that on board ourselves and discussed about keeping yourself safe and that includes during sexual health. (Depute head teacher, Dundee)

Regardless of what we consider appropriate, we cannot ignore the fact that 10 % of children will have their first sexual experience by the age of fourteen, and the median age of first intercourse is sixteen (Wight and Henderson, 2004). If we wish to protect children then it is important to discuss issues such as contraception with children. It is also important to recognise that the purpose of sex education is not to encourage young people to have sex but to delay sexual activity. There is good evidence from a number of European countries that an explicit SRE programme does not encourage young people to engage in sexual activity at younger age and that it may actually help to reduce the rate of teenage pregnancies (Burtney, 2000; Health Scotland, 2006).

The clitoris

The clitoris

Although homosexuality and contraception were raised as issues by many teachers interviewed as part of the Tayside research, it was the use of the term 'clitoris' in the *Living and Growing* programme and the SRE curriculum that caused the most discomfort. Teachers' unwillingness to use the term led some schools to take extraordinary steps to remove it from the curriculum.

> We were talking about the clitoris. We took that out of the little ones, we tippexed over it then photocopied the sheets, then we glazed over it here. That wasn't my decision, that was the head teacher. (Teacher, Primary 3–7, Perth & Kinross)

> … the staff were not keen on some of the elements, and part of their problem was that it wasn't their responsibility to do that, and there were bits of it that they think some of the words they feel are not appropriate, bit about the clitoris etc. They just think that it's nonsense that you have to go on about that, and they think it's all very well talking about parts, but that isn't a part that you can see. I actually had wipe it out because otherwise I would have had a riot on my hands. They were prepared to accept the rest of it but not that. So that was wiped out. (Headteacher Primary 1–3, Perth & Kinross)

> To be perfectly honest I still don't feel the need for it [the clitoris], although I can see they might investigate their bodies and think there is something freakish about them if they discover this extra bit and don't know what it is, but I just personally think it's just too young. I just don't think they need to know that at that stage. (Teacher, Primary 1–7, Perth & Kinross)

The reason for this concern is not immediately clear. The teachers interviewed seem very relaxed about naming all the other parts of the body including the 'penis', but had real difficulty naming the clitoris. One Depute Headteacher suggested that parents might be concerned if their girls came to them and said 'rubbing this feels good' but did not have the same concern about using the word penis.

[The staff] weren't happy about it all, I didn't think there was a need when they were only in primary to be talking about the clitoris and I know that, against what I've been saying, they take all for granted and so on but there is a bit of me says it will just go over their head if they are not ready to accept that word, but I can see where the staff are coming from and the staff that brought that up said they had little ones of their own and don't want them to be saying look mummy I have got this or I can feel good when I give this a rub. (Depute Headteacher, Dundee)

It is possible that the concern about the clitoris actually arises from the inability of teachers to explain the purpose of the clitoris without discussing sexual pleasure, unlike the penis which also has a non-sexual function. One interviewee said that, from her experience, parents had a particular problem with explaining the idea of sexual pleasure to their young children.

The main things that came from the parents and the one thing that we have removed from the programme is clitoris. That was a major issue with the parents…how do you explain sexual pleasure to a young child? I don't think it is appropriate. However I did not take that to the parents. I did not put my views on to the parents. If the parents were happy with that because that was the programme we would have to run with it. But the parents were not happy with that. They asked me the reason it was in. They could understand everything else and I explained that it was in because it was the only part of the sexual body that was purely for sexual pleasure and they were not happy with that. So we edited that out of the video at the moment. (Depute Headteacher, Dundee)

The fear of labelling the 'clitoris' and explaining its purpose may ultimately be a fear of discussing sex as a pleasurable act when the purpose of sexual health education in schools is to delay sexual activity and protect children from unwanted sexual advances. Such an emphasis may lead some teachers to emphasise the negative consequences of sex rather than sex as something which is pleasurable. There is clearly a fine line between encouraging young people to wait until they are both physically and emotionally ready for sexual relationships and portraying sex negatively.

Sex education in Scottish primary schools

Although the 'clitoris', 'contraception' and 'homosexuality' were the main areas of concern, a small number of interviewees raised other concerns that they found personally difficult to discuss. For example, one teacher had a personal problem discussing abortion and, even if it was raised by a child in her class, she would not discuss it, while another teacher felt very uncomfortable with the topic of masturbation. A significant number of teachers were also fearful of the questions that the children may bring to the class, particularly questions about oral sex.

One of the strengths of the *Sexuality and Relationship Training for Primary School Teachers* is that it provided teachers with practical ways of overcoming their concerns. For example, their fear of inappropriate questions being raised in the classroom can be overcome by using a question box. By using a question box, the teacher could decide whether an issue was appropriate to discuss with their class. Of course, it is not always possible to screen all questions; children may still raise questions in lessons even if there is a question box. In such circumstances it is very important for teachers to draw a line. As one interviewee said 'I am not a sex manual'. In most cases, teachers indicated if they felt the subject was too grown up for the child or inappropriate to discuss in front of the whole class, they would direct the child to their parents for answer.

Conclusion

If the Scottish Executive wants to reduce the number of teenage pregnancies in Scotland, it is essential that all teachers benefit from a comprehensive training programme that will enable them to become sexual health promoters in the classroom. Although all the teachers interviewed as part of the evaluation of Tayside Health Promotion's Sexuality and Relationship Training for Primary School Teachers had the benefits of training, there is no data on how many primary school teachers have access to training across all Scottish primary schools. Even in Tayside, where Tayside Health Promotion led the field in developing a training programme in collaboration with their local authority partners, many teaching staff have not had the opportunity to be trained as sexual health promoters. The survey of headteachers completed as part of this research found that a quarter of schools in Tayside did not have any staff trained for delivering SRE.

Pre-teen and teenage pregnancy

Despite this training gap, the Scottish Executive continues to emphasise the important role teachers and schools should have in promoting sexual health and the need for them to be properly trained:

> Schools have a crucial part to play in fostering healthy attitudes towards relationships, sex and sexuality in young people. All schools are expected to provide sex and relationships education. High-quality sex and relationships education should be delivered in an objective, balanced and sensitive manner by professionals who are trained for this role and who are able to support and complement the role of parents and carers as educators of children and young people. (Scottish Executive, 2005)

The comprehensive training of primary school teachers to deliver SRE is essential if sex education is going to be delivered consistently across all of Scotland's schools. Variability in the content of the SRE curriculum between schools will result in some young people being less prepared to negotiate with those making sexual demands of them and less able to say no to unwanted advances. However, to deliver SRE effectively teachers need to be supported, especially given that this is an area that many teachers are not comfortable with. The evaluation of the *Sexuality and Relationship Training for Primary Teachers* course suggests that training did significantly increase teachers' confidence and did enable them to deliver the curriculum more effectively. These findings echo the results of other research, for example, the SHARE evaluation found that teachers believed that collegiate support and the opportunity to familiarise themselves with the teaching materials, as well as overcoming their discomfort with the subject, were all benefits of training (Wight and Buston, 2003).

However, even after the training, aspects of the curriculum still caused some concern amongst those interviewed. Labelling the 'clitoris' caused the greatest discomfort amongst those we interviewed and many schools took steps to remove it from their curriculum. Other subjects also caused some concern, particularly homosexuality and contraception. These concerns seem to stem from teachers not wanting, or believing that it was inappropriate, to discuss the 'nitty gritty' details of sex with their pupils. Yet this may be exactly what is needed, if we are going to lower the rate of teenage pregnancy in Scotland.

References

Annetts, J. and Law, J. (2006) *Sex Education in Primary School in Tayside: An evaluation of sexuality and relationships training for primary teachers* Edinburgh: HMSO.

Burtney, E. (2000) *Teenage Sexuality in Scotland: Evidence into action* Edinburgh: HEBS.

Buston, K. and Hart, G. (2001) Heterosexism and homophobia in Scottish school sex education: Exploring the nature of the problem. *Journal of Adolescence* 24: 95–109.

Buston, K., Wight, D. and Scott, S. (2001) Difficulty and diversity: The context and practice of sex education. *British Journal of Sociology of Education* 22(3): 353–368.

Dunphy, R. (2000) *Sexual Politics: An introduction* Edinburgh: Edinburgh University Press.

Epstein, D. (2000) Sexualities and education: Catch 28. *Sexualities* 3(4): 387–39

Forrest, J., Souter, J. and Walker, S. (1994) *Personal Relationships and Developing Sexuality: A staff development resource for teachers* Glasgow: University of Strathclyde.

Health Scotland (2006) *The Place of Abstinence in Sex and Relationships Education in Scotland* Briefing Paper 1 Sexual Health and Wellbeing Learning Network. Edinburgh: Health Scotland.

Lewis, J. and Knijn, T. (2002) The politics of sex education policy in England and Wales and the Netherlands since the 1980s. *Journal of Social Policy* 31(4): 669–694.

Scottish Executive (2000a) *Report on the Working Group on Sex Education in Scottish Schools* Edinburgh: HMSO.

Scottish Executive (2000b) *Health Education: Guide for teachers and managers* Edinburgh: HMSO.

Scottish Executive (2001) *Sex Education in Scottish Schools: A guide for parents and carers* Edinburgh: HMSO.

Scottish Executive (2002) *Constructing the Problem, Constructing the Solutions: Young people's health and wellbeing in Scottish Executive Policies* Edinburgh: HMSO.

Scottish Executive (2003) *Enhancing Sexual Wellbeing in Scotland: A sexual health and relationship strategy* Consultation Paper. Edinburgh: Scottish Executive.

Scottish Executive (2005) *Respect and Responsibility: Strategy and action plan for improving sexual health* Edinburgh: HMSO.

Wallis, A. and Van Every, J. (2000) Sexuality in the primary school. *Sexualities* 3(4): 409–423.

Weis, D. (1999) Interpersonal heterosexual behaviour. In Koch, P. B. and Weis, D. L. (eds) *Sexuality in America* New York: Continuum.

Pre-teen and teenage pregnancy

Wight, D., Raab, G., Henderson, M., Abraham, C., Buston, K., Hart, G. and Scott, S. (2002) Limits of teacher delivered sex education: Interim behavioural outcomes from randomised trial. *British Medical Journal* 324: 1430.

Wight, D. and Buston, K. (2003) Meeting needs but not changing goals: Evaluation of in-service teacher training for sex education. *Oxford Review of Education* 29(4): 521–543.

Wight, D. and Henderson, M. (2004) The diversity of young people's hetero-sexual behaviour. In Burtney, E. and Duffy, M. (eds) *Young People and Sexual Health: Individual, social, and policy contexts* Basingstoke: Palgrave MacMillan: 15–33.

Young, I. (2004) Exploring the role of schools in sexual health promotion. In Burtney, E. and Duffy, M. (eds) *Young People and Sexual Health: Individual, social, and policy contexts* Basingstoke: Palgrave MacMillan: 521–43.

Chapter 7

Leanne: a snapshot of teenage sexual experience
Elizabeth Kennedy

In this chapter, we reproduce verbatim a case study presentation made by Elizabeth Kennedy to The Corner young people's health and information centre in Dundee on 21 September 2006. The case study presentation provides a candid account of the experience of a young woman from the age of thirteen to her last meeting with Elizabeth at the age of eighteen – a snapshot of life as a young person in Dundee, which has the highest rates of teenage pregnancy in Scotland. (See Chapter 5 for further explanation of the various contraceptives mentioned.)

Work at The Corner

Hi. Thank you for asking me to talk here today.

My name is Liz Kennedy and I am an Associate Specialist in Family Planning in Tayside. I have been working with The Corner since its inception ten years ago and continue to provide clinical care.

The doctors and the nurses in The Corner see over 6,000 clients per year. The young people attend for a variety of reasons – to obtain Emergency Hormonal Contraception (EHC), for first prescription of the Combined Pill, the Progestogen-Only Pill, Depo-Provera (the injectable contraceptive) and for repeat issue of all of these methods.

They also attend for counselling for insertion of Implanon (the subdermal rod), for counselling for IUD or IUS (commonly called 'coils'). We cannot offer these procedures within The Corner but we can tell people about them. And they attend for counselling regarding unplanned pregnancy and referral for termination of pregnancy if that is their decision.

Pre-teen and teenage pregnancy

The project workers at The Corner have been trained in-house, by the nurses and myself, to offer pregnancy tests and to issue condoms with instructions and advice. Our service is called 'Bodymatters' and, while completely integrated into The Corner, we have regular clinical and management meetings to discuss specific issues.

The drop-in clinics where all these young people are seen are held during the time The Corner is open, from 12 noon to 5pm each weekday and from 1pm to 4pm on Saturdays. In addition a doctor is available from 3pm to 5.30pm on Mondays and from 1pm to 3pm on Saturdays. We see our clients in two private rooms at the rear of the main concourse. These are furnished in a non-clinical way but we have dedicated cupboards and filing cabinets to stock our drugs and client notes. There are toilet facilities and a sluice area beside the consultation rooms.

So that I can describe what we do I have decided to present a case history. This is a real client and a real story but is completely anonymised. There are no typical clients – every client is an individual.

The case study

Case study

I first saw Leanne about six years ago.

She had presented to The Corner nurse requesting emergency hormonal contraceptive pills. At this time she was just under thirteen years old.

We had, and have, a policy whereby the doctor sees all clients under thirteen years old. This policy has been written down and refined since my original consultation with Leanne. We now have specific guidelines and specific forms to complete to ensure all child protection issues are covered. However, at that time we had verbal procedures in place to ensure the client was looked after properly.

Leanne was a small thin girl with long dark hair – highlighted with blonde – who sat in the corner of one of our sofas. She looked up at me and gave me a small smile when I came in. I explained who I was and said that the nurse had asked me to see her.

She made eye contact again but she didn't say anything. I said I wondered how I could help her. She looked up and said 'Eh'm

Leanne: a snapshot of teenage sexual experience

here for the morning after pill. The nurse said eh had to see you first.' I said 'That's right, I like to see all the clients under thirteen years and have a chat with them about having sex, about who they are having sex with and to see if they want to have sex.'

'Do you mind if I ask you some questions?'

'No – on you go,' she said.

'Can you tell me when you had sex?'

'Last night about nine o'clock'.

'Is this your first time?'

'Naw – I've been having sex since I started senior school'.

'So, how many partners have you had?'

'Three now – this lad is the fourth.'

'And do you quite like having sex?'

'It's OK.'

'Do you ever get forced into it?'

'No, it's what they want and I don't mind. We use condoms, but this one burst'.

'What ages are your partners?'

'They are all in my class at school'

Just to digress here, you might think that there is no way I could remember all the things she said. However, this was a memorable client as she was so young when I first saw her. Also, I keep very full notes and often write down snatches of dialogue which I find helps me remember the client when I next see them.

I then asked her about drinking.

*'Yes, sometimes when I go to parties but I'm never "out of it".
I'd no sleep wi' just anyone.'*

'Can you talk to your Mum?'

'No, she'd go ballistic. She's got problems of her own anyway.'

'Anyone else?'

'Well, I can talk to my big cousin, she's nineteen and she's OK about things.'

I was still wondering to myself why this client had started her sexual life so young, so I tried again.

Pre-teen and teenage pregnancy

'How do you feel having sex, do you enjoy it?'

She thought a bit. 'I don't really feel anything. It's not sore, like, if that's what you mean.'

I was concerned about Leanne, yet she was competent, seemed to understand what she was doing and could talk to an adult.

'OK,' I said. 'Let's see about the emergency pills.' This I felt was in the best interests of the client and the reason she had presented.

We talked about EHC and I explained how it worked and how effective it was. I then got some water and watched her take the first tablet. Although we now are able to give EHC as a single dose, six years ago we had to give tablets to be given at a 12 hour interval. I impressed on Leanne how important it was to take the rest of the tablets in 12 hours and to return if her period didn't come when expected.

I asked her about a regular form of contraception but she said she didn't want to go on the pill.

'What about some other method.'

'No, its alright.'

'Well, I'll give you a leaflet … What about condoms?'

'I got some from the other woman.' (She meant the nurse)

Leanne: a snapshot of teenage sexual experience

'Do you know about the types of infection you can get from having sex?'

'Eh, we got it at school.'

I asked her to come back and speak to one of the nurses but by this time her eyes had completely glazed over and I knew it was time to finish.

We have to give our clients so much information in a consultation that it is no wonder they cannot remember what they have been told. I know I would have difficulty and my brain is supposed to be mature.

I didn't see Leanne again until she was just over fourteen years old.

I gave my usual opening 'Oh, hi, my name is Liz Kennedy, I'm one of the doctors here. I don't know if you remember me but I saw you about eighteen/twelve months ago. What can I help you with today?'

She smiled a bit at me and seemed to remember.

'I need the morning after pill.'

We went through her story. She had now been going out with Rick, a boy in the year above her at school, for three months.

'He's really nice'

'Any other partners?'

'No, just him.'

'Remember when you were here last time you told me about other boys you had been with – what happened?'

'I stopped all that, didn't really like it anyway.'

So we went over the emergency contraception again. I asked her about a more regular contraception.

'Well, I've heard the pill makes you fat.'

We talked about that misapprehension but still she didn't want anything but condoms.

I suggested she go for a check up at the GU clinic and offered to make her an appointment. She said she would make one herself.

I was happier at that consultation. We had gone over things again. She now seemed to be in a good relationship but she was still fourteen and at risk of pregnancy and STD.

* * *

About ten months later, one of the nurses brought in a set of notes to me.

Pre-teen and teenage pregnancy

'I'm a bit worried about this girl – she has been in for emergency contraception six times in the last six months and I can't get her to consider doing anything safer.' It was Leanne. 'Do you think she will come and talk to me?'

She managed to avoid me for a few weeks but eventually, one Monday, I saw her. She had changed. Her hair was short and spikey, she had piercings and looked about twenty years old.

I explained that we didn't know the long-term effects of using EHC frequently and while we didn't think there were any problems about using a high dose of hormone regularly we didn't know for sure.

She considered that.

'Yeah, the nurses have said that but it always seems easier just to use condoms and get the pills when I need them.'

She was not with Rick any more.

'He dumped me.'

She had several other short-term partners. She usually used condoms but not always.

'Can you still talk to your big cousin?'

'Yes, I don't see her so much now. My mum got depression and kicked me out. She couldn't cope with me going out so much. I stay with my Gran now but she lives on the other side of Dundee.'

'Do you speak to your Gran?'

'Yes, sometimes, she doesn't mind me going out at night.'

'So how about thinking of the pill, or the injection or something else?'

'Well, OK, I guess I could try the pill.'

We went on to a full history, I checked her weight and blood pressure and counselled her about taking the pill. She was a smoker and we talked about smoking and health problems – again the concern with weight.

'I won't put weight on will I?'

She went away with condoms, three months' supply of the pill and a promise to talk to her cousin and maybe her Gran. The nurses and I were quite pleased we had seemed to 'sort things out'.

* * *

Leanne: a snapshot of teenage sexual experience

Leanne came back to see us in six weeks. She complained that she was bleeding all the time and had put on weight. I was concerned about the bleeding. She was at risk of STD especially chlamydia. She seemed to be taking her pill correctly.

'Tell me what's happening.'

'Oh, I'm bleeding all the time and its sore when I have sex.'

She had not made the GU clinic appointment we had suggested at a previous visit. We talked about STDs and that chlamydia was very common. I told her we couldn't test her at The Corner and made her an appointment at the GU clinic.

* * *

Two months later Leanne returned. Her bleeding had stopped shortly after her last visit so she didn't go to her appointment at the clinic. She didn't reckon she needed the pill anymore as she was not seeing anyone. So she stopped it. As she had now had no period for two months, a friend had thought she should come in for a pregnancy test. The test was positive. She was fifteen years old.

'I can't cope with a baby.'

We went through her options and counselled her about the process of a termination of pregnancy. She was quite composed and seemed to understand her choices and what she was going to do.

She decided to try Depo Provera after the termination was over. I made her appointment for her and gave her all the necessary documents and arranged for her to come back two weeks after the termination to see how she was and to find out how the Depo was suiting her.

Some time later, I received a letter from the hospital stating that she had been for her termination and they had given her an injection of Depo before she left the ward. The letter also said she had been tested for chlamydia – standard procedure – and found positive. She had been given antibiotic treatment. She was planning to attend The Corner for further contraception.

* * *

Leanne returned eventually. She wanted emergency contraception. She didn't like the Depo – it had made her bleed and put on weight. She didn't reckon she needed contraception anyway as 'Eh'm no with anyone.' However, she had had sex last night with a boy she knew, didn't use condoms and was by now not protected by the Depo. We talked again mainly about the emergency pill, future contraception and risk of STD. We talked about herself and how she felt. 'OK,' she said. She thought it might be a good idea to start on the pill again and get another STD check.

She went away after taking the emergency pill, getting three months' supply of a different sort of pill and a card to remind her to phone the GU clinic. I felt dispirited, I wondered how Leanne was really feeling. Her life was so full of difficulties. She had had a termination and an STD. Her mother was still depressed and she was staying with her Gran. She had changed schools as she had not been attending her old school, but she didn't like her new school. Her attempts at finding love had not worked. Her life seemed blighted before it had really started

However, much to my delight she stayed on the pill. We saw her three times for more pills and then lost touch with her.

* * *

I saw Leanne just the other day. She came into my other clinic for an Implanon insertion. She had been seen by one of the nurses in a local GP clinic, who had made out new notes for her, counselled her about Implanon and arranged for her to attend me for insertion.

I remembered her straightaway and she recognised me. During the procedure she chatted about herself. She is now over eighteen years old. She had continued on the pill, attending her GP for it as she felt she had 'grown out of' The Corner. 'It's full of kids.'

She had gone to college to sit her highers and was now going to start a nursing course – hence the reason she wanted a reliable long-term contraceptive. 'I'm really pleased to see you again. I was always so worried about you when you were younger and I saw you at The Corner. What changed?' She shook her head, 'I don't really know. I was really stupid back then, wasn't I?'

* * *

Leanne: a snapshot of teenage sexual experience

No conclusions

So, that's Leanne's story. No answers but loads of questions:
- Why had she taken all these risks?
- Why had she been unable to act on information and advice?
- Would she be permanently damaged by her experiences as a young teenager?
- Could we have done anything different?
- Perhaps if she had a more stable background...
- Perhaps if she had more self esteem...
- Perhaps if we had been able to offer more integrated care...

I have a dream, you know, which involves a large central building containing family planning and sexual health services for all ages including termination services, all STD screening, treatment and partner notification and full range of contraceptives. Men and women could attend, the stigma would be taken out of sexual issues and everything would be under one roof.

Would this have changed the course of Leanne's journey? Would it help those who follow?

I don't know!

Chapter 8
Local initiatives: A sexual health doctor's experience

Dianna Reed

Strategies to reduce teenage pregnancy and promote sexual health in the under 25s are currently a hot political topic. These areas are the focus of the Sexual Health Strategy and various approaches are already underway to tackle them (NHS Tayside, 2005).

Sexual activity amongst young people has been gradually increasing since the 1960s. This has been particularly marked amongst teenagers. The proportion of young people who have sexual intercourse before the age of sixteen is rising (Wright *et al.*, 2000) and many studies have shown that this is often associated with regret (Johnson *et al.*, 1994; Dickson *et al.*, 1998). This chapter discusses strategies to address this problem and looks more closely at the problems with one particular initiative in Angus.

Statistics for Tayside

Statistics for Tayside

Dundee, Angus, Perth and Kinross are all areas within Tayside. The teenage pregnancy rate in Tayside has been one of the highest in Scotland for a number of years. In particular, Dundee City Council had the highest teenage pregnancy rate of 64.4 per 1000 women aged thirteen to nineteen in 2003–4 (National Services Scotland, 2006). This was set against a background rate of 42.2 per 1000 for Scotland as a whole.

In Angus, Perth and Kinross, the frequency of pregnancies occurring in the thirteen- to fifteen-year-old age groups remained relatively static between 1994 and 2002, averaging five to nine per 1000 in Perth and five to 14 per 1000 in Angus. The rate increased slightly in 2003–4 and this was most marked in Angus.

In Dundee City the rates have been higher in the same age group, averaging 14 to 20 per 1000 between 1994 and 2002. Although there has been a gradual downward trend over this time, there was an increase in 2003–4 from the previous year (Easton, 2006).

Pre-teen and teenage pregnancy

There is an association with social deprivation and teenage conception rates and the rates are highest in areas with the highest levels of deprivation (Easton, 2006).

**Regretted
sexual activity**

Regretted sexual activity

The figures for teenage pregnancy merely highlight the problems that need addressing. Firstly, we can look at teenage attitudes towards sex.

Some research has been done surrounding the issue of regretted sexual intercourse amongst teenagers. One such study, by Wright *et al.* (2000) involved a large scale survey of all third year pupils in 24 non-denominational state secondary schools in East Scotland, as part of a sex education trial. The survey was conducted by a questionnaire administered under exam conditions, in the absence of teaching staff. Consent was obtained from both young people and their parents. The results showed that 18% of boys and 15.4% of girls had experienced heterosexual intercourse by the time they had reached the age of fourteen. Three-quarters of all respondents stated that their first experience had occurred after their thirteenth birthday. Worryingly, this would suggest that a sizable minority were under thirteen at the time. Perhaps equally disconcerting is that only 60% reported using condoms and 19% used no contraception at all. These figures were similar for the most recent episode of intercourse, implying that risk-taking behaviour continues over time.

Approximately 20% of all girls reported that they had been under some kind of pressure to have sex at first and most recent intercourse. This compared with less than 10% of boys. In addition, only two-fifths of all pupils felt that first intercourse occurred at 'about the right time'. Approximately one-third of both boys and girls felt that it happened too early. In contrast to the teenage pregnancy rate in Dundee, there seemed to be no association between sexual activity, regret and social class. Looking at international variations in teenage pregnancy, even the most affluent areas of the UK have a higher rates than the national average for the Netherlands and France (Wellings *et al.*, 2001).

Interestingly, factors associated with regret in girls were feelings of being 'pressured', not having planned intercourse and where there were intense levels of parental monitoring. However,

according to Wright *et al.* (2000) it would seem that these fa
do not necessarily act as a deterrent.

Sexual competence

The relationship between young age at first sex, pregnancy and STDs may be at least partly explained by lack of sexual competence. Competence is defined by measurements of regret, willingness, autonomy and appropriate use of contraception (Wellings *et al.*, 2001). The National Survey of Sexual Attitudes and Lifestyles (NATSAL) conducted interviews with people aged sixteen to forty-four years. It assessed patterns of sexual behaviour in Britain in 2000. This showed that lack of sexual competence increases with decreasing age of first intercourse (Macdowall *et al.*, 2006). Indeed, 91% of girls and 67% of boys were 'not competent at first intercourse'. An alternative approach may be working with young people to increase their self-esteem and thereby improving their negotiating skills.

What can be done?

The difficulty of tackling this problem is immense. The issues can be addressed from many angles and here we look at two – sex education and the provision of young people's sexual health clinics.

Sex education

Strategies to increase the age of first intercourse could be employed, perhaps by educating teenagers as to the drawbacks of sex at a young age. Sex education programmes within schools have always been a contentious issue on both religious and moral grounds.

Various studies have been undertaken to ascertain whether sex education has any effect on age of first intercourse. To date, Baldo *et al.* (1993) claim that no studies have shown that it leads to earlier or increased sexual activity. Promisingly, some studies have shown that it leads to a delay in sexual activity. In 1999, a survey of adolescent attitudes towards sex found that adolescents who were well informed about sexual health were less likely to be influenced by peer pressure or to be sexually active (Baruck, 1999). Given that early sexual initiation is an important factor in teenage pregnancy and sexually transmitted diseases (STDs), any strategy that can delay the onset would seem appropriate. Abstinence programmes, for example, are commonplace in parts of the United States. However, as the British Medical Association (2003) highlights, these programmes have had no demonstrable effect on delaying sexual activity or reducing teenage pregnancy. Perhaps young people just don't want this approach.

Sexual health clinics

Young people's sexual health clinics

Working within the field of young people's sexual health can produce a whole range of emotions. It can be challenging and rewarding but equally frustrating at times. Our role is usually one of damage limitation.

In my experience few people come to the clinics before they become sexually active. Arguably, this is too late a stage to look at delaying first intercourse. However, as suggested previously and noted by Oakley *et al.* (1995), perhaps young people may want more practical guidance about their sexual health rather than emphasising the physical or moral disadvantages. This is an area to which the sexual health clinic lends itself well. However, providing a sexual health and family planning service only addresses part of the problem. Only if people are motivated to attend can we tailor the service to meet their current needs.

Sexual health clinics in Scotland

Currently in Scotland there are vast regional variations in the organisation of young people's sexual health services.

Dundee has a comprehensive service known as The Corner aimed at the under twenty-fives. This was set up in 1996 and has premises in the town centre. It is open six days a week and has two main purposes. It is staffed by nurses trained in family planning and sexual health, who predominantly provide contraception and health advice. In addition, there are a number of project workers who meet other needs. For example, they can provide counselling and advice on social problems. Close links have been created with social work and mental health services in the area. Analysing figures for April 2005 to March 2006, 29% of attendees at The Corner were aged eleven to fifteen years. A further 55% were aged sixteen to twenty and only 16% were over twenty-one. Approximately 50 to 60% of these attendances were for sexual health purposes (Craven, 2006). Despite there being this well established service in Dundee, the teenage pregnancy rate for the area is still very high, but there has been a decreasing trend over the past ten years indicating that there may have been a positive effect.

Perth currently has four youth clinics a week. Two are held in a health centre in central Perth and the other two are held in Blairgowrie at school lunch times. Other cities in Scotland are not so fortunate. Aberdeen has two young persons' clinics a week and no peripheral provision of service at present.

Edinburgh has the benefit of the Healthy Respect project which is funded to provide youth clinics all over Lothian (Healthy Respect Services, 2006). This area of Scotland is well supplied. The main aim is to encourage young people to enjoy healthy and respectful relationships.

The Glasgow area is also well supplied. There are various models, both around the city and in more peripheral locations. The Sandyford Initiative offers sexual health services to all ages. This incorporates both the family planning services and GU medicine under one roof. Another service running in the east end of Glasgow is known as H4U. This is separately funded and offers a holistic range of information on health and dealing with social problems. There are a variety of independent services across the Greater Glasgow and Clyde area to cover the places where access to the more centralised services may be difficult (NHS, 2006).

Angus: The challenge of reaching the under 16s

Reaching the under 16s

For the last four years the young people's sexual health clinic in Angus has been running once a week on a Tuesday afternoon. This has been a drop-in service for the under twenty-fives. In addition, Young People's Health Workers came in post in 2004. They are based in various secondary schools in Angus. One of their primary objectives is health promotion in schools, the aim being to support, deliver and evaluate relevant general wellbeing and sexual health services in Angus. In addition to supporting sex education in schools, there are weekly clinics in Arbroath Infirmary. In addition, they run a mobile service to supply the outlying areas. This is in the form of a well-equipped campervan known as the Youthbytes Bus.

Pre-teen and teenage pregnancy

It delivers general health, sexual health advice, emergency contraception and pregnancy testing to the more rural areas of Angus. The young people using this service would otherwise have difficulty accessing the clinics in the main towns.

Over many years of working in Angus it became apparent that many of our young people's clinics were attended by over sixteens, with under sixteens considerably less well represented. Given the proportions of those who become sexually active much earlier, this seemed a little incongruous. This was partly thought to be due to the timing of the clinic which was predominantly in school hours. Although a relatively open door policy for people to drop in straight after school was operating, this was not well advertised.

Improving take-up

A strategy to improve take-up

This issue was discussed with the Tayside Health Promotion department in an attempt to create a plan to improve access and encourage more school age children to attend. It was decided to run a 'mock family planning/sexual health clinic', with the following aims and objectives.

Aims

- To raise awareness of contraception and sexual health services for young people in Arbroath.
- To promote young people's access to contraception and sexual health services when and where appropriate.
- To work together with young people, school nurses, teaching staff and Young People's Health Workers with a view to improving the sexual health of teenagers in this area.

Objectives

- To promote the young people's drop-in clinic at the Abbey Health Centre.
- To introduce the medical, nursing and reception staff running the family planning clinic to pupils attending Arbroath Academy.
- To disseminate information regarding the way in which confidential client information is collected and recorded.
- To promote the confidential nature of the service and non-judgemental attitude of the staff.
- To provide up-to-date, relevant information about different methods of contraception and sexually transmitted diseases.

A sexual health doctor's perspective

- To advertise the services provided at the clinic.

- To promote a friendly and accessible service to the clientele.

A mock clinic was set up in the Abbey Health Centre, Arbroath. There was a number of staff involved, including myself, the family planning clinic nurse, the Arbroath Young People's Health Worker, the school guidance teacher and the school nurse.

Firstly, the school guidance teacher sent a note out to the parents for purposes of consent. There were no refusals. Pupils in the second (S2) and third (S3) years of an Arbroath secondary school aged between twelve and fourteen years, were invited to attend the clinic to gain knowledge of the premises and types of services available. Three separate year groups were invited in order to ascertain which year gained the most from the experience. Four groups, comprising approximately 12 to 16 pupils, attended over a period of two days in October and November 2005. Initially, they were introduced to the reception, medical and nursing staff and shown how to register at the clinic. The issue of confidentiality was discussed and the purposes of record keeping were explained.

Following this introduction, the pupils were divided into two smaller groups and shown into the consulting rooms. These were set up with two stations.

Station 1

This station consisted of a set of mock case notes to show the type of questions routinely asked during a consultation. This was an attempt to demonstrate how and why information is collected and recorded. This was on an informal basis and the pupils were encouraged to ask questions. Some of the myths surrounding sex and contraception were explored.

Station 2

This station consisted of examples of various types of contraception, pictures of STDs and equipment used in the clinics. This included swabs, laboratory sample bottles and a speculum. The corresponding leaflets were available to peruse. A member of staff was available in each room to demonstrate some of the methods and answer any questions.

At the end of each clinic visit, evaluation forms were distributed to all the pupils. They were encouraged to complete these and return them before leaving. The aim of the evaluation form was to determine the pupils' view of the validity of the exercise. Information was collected anonymously. This consisted of both open and closed questions with a space for comments or further questions that could be answered by the teaching staff at a later date in a life skills lesson at school. The only demographic information requested was their age and year group. A copy of the questionnaire can be found at the end of the chapter.

The questionnaires were collated and analysed and the results are presented in Table 8.1 below.

Table 8.1

Questionnaire result

AGE GROUP	12	13	14
MALES	0	8	9
FEMALES	1	7	20
PUPILS FEELING VISIT WAS USEFUL	1	15	29
PUPILS FEELING VISIT WAS NOT USEFUL			
PUPILS WITH PRIOR KNOWLEDGE OF CLINIC		9	14
PUPILS WITH NO PRIOR KNOWLEDGE OF CLINIC	1	6	15
PUPILS WHO THOUGHT VISIT WOULD BE USEFUL FOR OTHERS	1	13	28
PUPILS WHO THOUGHT VISIT WOULD NOT BE USEFUL FOR OTHERS			
PUPILS THINKING CLINIC TIME SHOULD BE EXTENDED	1	7	21
PUPILS THINKING CLINIC TIME DOES NOT NEED TO CHANGE		7	9
PUPILS WHO WOULD HAVE LIKED MORE INFORMATION			5

In total, 44 pupils out of a possible 257 across S2 and S3, came to visit the clinic over two separate days. This equated to 17% of the school years. The visit was not compulsory. A further eight pupils requested to come initially and later declined to come on the day.

A sexual health doctor's perspective

Analysing the data from this table, it has been shown that everyone who came found the visit useful. Only three pupils stated they 'did not know' whether the exercise would be useful to others. The remaining 41 thought that it almost certainly would be beneficial. Opinions on whether the clinic opening hours should be extended varied in the different age groups.

Of those who came, 50% of thirteen-year-olds thought that the clinic hours were fine as they were and 50% thought they should be increased. This compared with the fourteen-year-old age group where 30% felt that the current clinic times were appropriate and 70% thought that the clinic closed too early.

Five pupils stated that they would have liked more information. Unfortunately, none of them filled out the part of the questionnaire asking what this might have been.

Discussion points

Looking at these results, it would seem that older pupils perceived greater gain from extending the current clinic time. There may be differing explanations for this. Perhaps the issues raised and discussed were more relevant to this particular age group, since statistically more S3s are likely to be sexually active than S2s. Furthermore, it is possible that only the highly motivated pupils chose to come to the clinic. Perhaps this self-selected group are more likely to display sexual competence than those who chose not to come.

There may have been some area of the mock clinic that could have been done differently to encourage the visitors to ask more questions. Little time was available for any personal, one-to-one questions to be answered. It was hoped that the visit would promote further discussion in the life skills classes held within the school. A further aim of this was to disseminate information to the pupils who did not have the opportunity to attend. Perhaps this could be achieved by process of peer education. Unfortunately, the practical difficulties entailed with follow up were that the school guidance staff member who took part in organising the project moved to a different school shortly after completion, naturally causing problems with continuity.

Initially, three different year groups were invited to attend, including S4 pupils. Unfortunately, due to unforeseen circumstances, the third planned day had to be cancelled due to staff shortages. This particular day would have involved the fourth year. This year group might have gained more from the experience and been more confident about asking questions.

A further obvious limitation of this project was that only 17% of the pupils from the two school years were able to come. The reasons for this will be discussed later.

Outcomes and barriers to implementing changes

All the pupils who visited the clinic over the two-day period found the experience worthwhile. A large majority of pupils stated that they would have liked to see an extension of the current clinic hours. The youth clinic drop-in facility was open from 2pm until 4pm on a Tuesday afternoon. Following this, the opening hours were extended from 2pm until 5.30pm. This now involves the Young People's Health Worker working from 4pm to 5.30pm with the doctor available until 4.45pm.

Unfortunately, this extension did not take place until August 2006. This meant there was a time lapse of ten months from when the project work was undertaken. Reasons included a number of staff changes in conjunction with funding issues. The family planning/sexual health service and the young people's health project are funded separately. Furthermore, an extension of reception cover had to be secured.

Analysing the attendance figures for the period August 2005 to August 2006, only 14% of our clientele were under sixteen. This has risen to 16% for the period from when the clinic was extended until the present time. It is too early to assess whether that change in clinic time will have a significant effect on the number of attendances in the long term.

The time lapse between the 'mock clinic' and the expansion of opening hours may have had a negative effect on the attendance figures. Furthermore, the subject of sexual health only comes around once a year in the life skills classes and as such, has not been top of the agenda recently. However, the Young People's Health Workers did advertise the clinic extension within the school. Ideally, advertising would be in the local press. However, at present there is no budget for this.

Follow-up work and conclusions

The concept of a mock clinic seemed to be a useful exercise for all the pupils, school and clinic staff involved because it raised the opportunity to assess and meet the needs of young people. It was anticipated that this would be repeated this year, perhaps with a different year group and another secondary school

Regrettably, this process is fraught with difficulty. In order to set up the mock clinic actual clinic rooms were used. These rooms are multidisciplinary which means they are only available for a mock clinic when either a young persons' or general family planning/sexual health clinic would otherwise be running. Therefore, two clinics had to be cancelled to accommodate the mock clinic. This has the potential to increase waiting times to the detriment of other clients. In addition, the project has to run during school hours. Given the limited accommodation within the clinic, only a relatively small number of pupils could be seen at any one time. This serves to restrict the number of pupils who can have the opportunity to visit from any given school year.

Although there seems no doubt that the concept of the mock clinic was well received and felt to be worthwhile by all those concerned, it remains to be seen whether the number of school age attendees at the young persons' youth clinic increases. Ultimately, more research is needed to assess ways of improving the sexual health of the youth of today.

Acknowledgements

I would like to thank: the reception and nursing staff who participated in the project; the Young People's Health Workers who helped with the project and have allowed the clinics to be extended; my colleagues in family planning in Perth, Dundee, Aberdeen, Glasgow and Edinburgh for information regarding youth clinics in their respective areas and the Department of Public Health in Tayside for the local statistics on teenage pregnancy.

Pre-teen and teenage pregnancy

References

Baldo, M., Aggleton, P. and Slutkin, G. (1993) Does sex education lead to earlier or increased sexual activity in youth? *International Conference on AIDS* 9: 792.

Baruck, R. (1999) Teenage sexual behaviour: Attitudes towards and declared sexual activity. *British Journal of Family Planning* 24: 145–148.

Craven, D. (2006) *The Corner Statistics* Dundee: NHS Tayside.

Dickson, N., Paul, C., Herbison, P. and Silva, P. (1998) First sexual intercourse: Age, coercion, and later regrets reported by a birth cohort. *British Medical Journal* 316: 29–33.

Easton, P. (2006) *Population Profile for Inequalities: Strategy Summary of Main Findings, Phase 3* Dundee: NHS Tayside.

Healthy Respect (2006) *Services Directory*. Available at http://www.healthyrespect.org.uk/ (accessed November 2006)

Johnson, A.M., Wadsworth, J., Wellings, K., Field, J. and Bradshaw, S. (1994) *Sexual Attitudes and Lifestyles*. London: Blackwell Scientific.

Macdowall, W., Wellings, K., Mercer, C.H., Nanchahal, K., Copas, A.J., McManus, S., Fenton, K.A., Erens, B. and Johnson, A.M. (2006) Learning about sex: Results from NATSAL 2000. *Health Education and Behaviour* 33(6): 802–811.

National Services Scotland (2006) *Scottish Health Statistics: Teenage Pregnancy*. http://www.isdscotland.org/isd/2669.html (accessed October 2006).

NHS (2006) Sexual Health and Relationships website: http://www.yoursexualhealth.org.uk/sexualwellbeing.php. (accessed November 2006).

Oakley, A., Fullerton, D. and Holland, J. (1995) Sexual health education interventions for young people: A methodological review. *British Medical Journal* 310: 158–162.

The Sexual Health Strategy Group (2005) *Tayside Sexual Health and Relationships Strategy* Dundee: NHS Tayside. Available at http://www.nhstayside.scot.uk (accessed May 2007).

Wellings, K., Nanchahal, K., Macdowall, W., McManus, S., Erens, B. and Mercer, C.H, (2001) Sexual behaviour in Britain: Early heterosexual experience. *The Lancet* 358: 1843–1845.

Wright, D., Henderson, M., Raab, G., Abraham, C., Buston, K. and Scott, S. (2000) Extent of regretted sexual intercourse among young teenagers in Scotland: A cross-sectional survey. *British Medical Journal* 320(7244): 1243–1244.

Chapter 9
The future's fine – or is it?
June L. Leishman
James Moir

The health and wellbeing of young people has always been complex and has always posed challenges for societies. Twenty-first century youth remains equally complex and challenging. Risk-taking behaviours in young people are not a new phenomenon. The culture of alcohol consumption, drug taking, crime and violence and sex is a reality for young people in today's world. However, the discussions and debates in this book have shown that the short- and long-term consequences of early age sexual activity that presents difficulties for the young person, their families and society remain at crisis level in the twenty-first century.

Despite some reduction in the figures, the UK continues to have one of the highest pre-teen and teenage pregnancy rates in western civilised society. It also has one of the highest rates of legalised abortion in teenagers. Associated with sexual activity are the alarming increases in sexually transmitted diseases, HIV and AIDS. In developed countries such as the UK, there is a close correlation between social deprivation and adolescent pregnancy and it is not uncommon for pregnant adolescent girls to experience abuse and maltreatment. Adolescent childbearing is commonly associated with negative long-term effects for the mothers, including future adolescent births, adverse socio-economic conditions, fractured education and poor earning capacity.

Evidence of the negative health consequences of early age pregnancy is well documented in policy documents, academic publications and research reports, with increased risks identified for both the pregnant mother and her child. Coupled with this is the psychological impact of early pregnancy on young people, which frequently includes stress, depression and sometimes suicide.

Current government policy advocates a national campaign to improve understanding and change behaviour. It seeks to co-ordinate action at local and national levels and across service providers. It also looks to improve teenage pregnancy prevention through education and access to contraception, with a particular focus on at risk groups and young males.

Sex education and adolescent-focused healthcare provision are key to addressing this problem. Teachers of sex education, whether professional teachers or healthcare professionals, should be adequately prepared for this role. It is evident from the discussions in this book that the curriculum for SRE is delivered inconsistently across schools. This is problematic and will result in many young people receiving poor SRE education and limited information. The educators need to be well informed about sex, sexuality and relationships, birth control and sexual and reproductive health and contraception, and they need to communicate that knowledge confidently, sensitively and without moralising.

Although this is a commonly shared view amongst academic commentators and teachers in the field of sex education, it is nonetheless an immensely challenging issue bound up with notions of the boundaries between adulthood and childhood. Whenever adults are involved in talking to teenagers about the problems of engaging in 'adult behaviour', with its risks, pleasures and high status, then morality and the relative status of adults and children complicate matters. Sexual behaviour, alcohol consumption and smoking are all put to children as health and welfare issues and often disassociated from the world of status and pleasure. The notion that these are activities that adults can engage in and that teenagers need to be 'educated' about can all too easily be seen to be patronising and controlling. For teenagers, sex and relationships education can put them in an uncomfortable position as needing to be educated given their non-adult status.

Moreover, it is easy for such education to lapse into talk about sex and relationships in a way that is divorced from teenagers' everyday lives and experiences. It is one thing to sit in a classroom and 'talk the talk', so to speak. Making this a meaningful activity is another matter, and perhaps greater thought needs to be given to how the issue of teenage pregnancy can be made more of a live issue. This immediately raises issues related to gender, contraception, interpersonal relationships and so on, as well as the meaning of sex in society today in addition to its relationship with alcohol and drugs. Such sociological matters broaden out education in this area and allow for some degree of self-reflection.

One aspect of this sort of reflection is the extent to which sexual behaviour and relationships are turned into psychological concerns and deliberate decisions. For example, the idea the informed choice about contraception may reduce teenage pregnancy rates privileges a belief in forethought and planned behaviour. This separation of thought and action pits reason against emotion and is disconnected from teenagers' experiences. If such matters were raised in a more reflective manner then this might open up the possibility of teenagers being more aware of the sorts of dilemmas and difficulties they face with respect to sexual relationships. Again, a grounding in the varied social practices that constitute the nature of being a teenager needs to be at the centre of sex education, rather than abstract discourse based on rational decision-making.

It is in this sense that a wider appreciation of the different sub-cultural aspects of being a teenager in this day and age needs to be included in educational programmes that deal with sexual behaviour and relationships. It has previously been noted that teenage pregnancy is more of an issue for those from lower socio-economic backgrounds. However, it is not exclusively a problem at this level and therefore educational programmes need to be tailored to the lived experience of teenagers from a variety of backgrounds. There is little doubt that sexual health education must deal not only with the prevention of teenage pregnancy but also the reality of it and incorporate this in educational programmes. This does not mean accepting the present rates of teenage pregnancy in Britain today but recognising that advice on the care and support available for teenage mothers and fathers should accompany any attempt to address the situation.

What we have tried to present in this collection of articles is enough material to give readers a handle on the multi-faceted nature of teenage pregnancy. It is not an issue that is going to go away and it is, as we have tried to show, bound up with a range of complex social, economic, cultural, biological and educational issues. It is not easy to disentangle and apportion the relative importance of these factors, nor would this be fruitful. The best way forward is to recognise the complexity of the issue and most importantly attempt to situate it in the world of actual practice, rather than in the world of classroom discussion.

We do not want to overstate this; there is a place for classroom discussion and for more traditional types of information-giving education. However, there has been limited success with this kind of approach and it is time for a different approach, or set of approaches. These need to be much broader than in the past to encompass the complex nature of sexual relationships and behaviour in today's world. Sex education need not be turned into some sort of sociological analysis, but there is a need for much greater awareness of issues such as gender, alcohol consumption and identity than has traditionally been included.

Sex education must not be associated in the eyes of teenagers with notions of power and control and being told what is best for them. This is not an easy thing to do – all forms of education can easily slip into self-fulfilling discourses that justify their own status as wisdom – but perhaps we can try to move in the direction of accepting teenage pregnancy as a twenty-first century reality, whilst still helping teenagers to reflect upon this issue in all its complexity as it affects both them and their communities.

Index